MISS! MISS!
Confessions of a West Country Teacher

'...is remarkable and fascinating memoir is reminiscent of Miss ...ad and Alison Uttley's *The Country Child*. I loved it.'

...er reminiscences are at one and the same time witty and sad, ...gnant and thought provoking but always making for compulsive ...ding.

Katie Fforde

Miss! Miss! is an engaging and wise account of Una Dowding's life ...teaching career told with love, compassion and understanding.

In this collection, interspersed with selections from her poetry, she ...lls incidents throughout her life, as student, teacher and mother, ...ng in the county of Gloucestershire.

Una Dowding, having herself as a child struggled with and ...vercome difficulties in learning to read because of dyslexia, a problem ...generally recognised by teachers in her own schooldays, regales ...with recollected incidents, sometimes touchingly funny or tear-...ingly sad which demonstrate a deep understanding of the need ...others to learn from an early age. One particularly sad account ...of an emotionally troubled child who was often locked out of ...house at night-time by the mother. Several humorous incidents ...onstrate how a deep need to learn was recognised and encouraged, ...instance, in the Polish child who scorned primary reading books ...was determined to read a very adult account of *The Sinking of the* ...*ic* from cover to cover.

Miss! Miss! certainly deserves to be read from cover to cover.

A book not just for teachers and parents, but for all readers who enjoy ...worthwhile read based upon true life.

Eugenie Summerfield
...nd novelist)

D0238043

MISS! MISS!

Confessions of a West Country Teacher

by

Una Dowding

ARTHUR H. STOCKWELL LTD
Torrs Park, Ilfracombe, Devon, EX34 8BA
Established 1898
www.ahstockwell.co.uk

British Library Cataloguing-in-Publication Data.
A catalogue record for this book is available
from the British Library.

ISBN 978-0-7223-4452-1
Printed in Great Britain by
Arthur H. Stockwell Ltd
Torrs Park   Ilfracombe
Devon EX34 8BA

It should be noted that children at play are not playing about; their games should be seen as their most serious-minded activity.

Montaigne, 1533–92

Always remember that every adult has been a child, but no child has ever been an adult.

L. C. Hauting, 1905–44

EARTH TO EARTH

A jewelled cradle holds me still
In Gloucestershire.

The buttercup and Dymock's daffodils
Layer the Springtime meadows with their gold,
With coral bird's-eye speckling the grass
And bluebells' sapphire haze beneath the trees.

My pearls are scattered on the Cotswold hills,
As rounded sheep strung out across the vale
Above the bubbling streams and cameo pools
Where hunts the darting, cobalt kingfisher.

My diamonds are the droplets of a dew
Borne upon a silvered, quivering web,
Live orbs of iridescent light
Set amongst the glistening ruby haws.

Across Sabina's deep carnelian flow
Lie Dean's majestic gnarled and emerald oaks
Encircling secret lakes, whose opalescent gleam
Reflects infinity beyond a topaz sky.

And I pray God I end my days
In Gloucestershire.

CONTENTS

All names of children have been altered, although incidents related actually occurred.

MAY GOD BLESS HER

Flames leapt into the darkening sky and sparks erupted in all directions as each file, book and sheaf of papers was added to the heart of the fire. Circling the conflagration, young women danced and yelled into the approaching night, as if set free from some sort of incarceration – as indeed they were, for this was the last night of the course. We were saying goodbye to two intensive years of study, tortuous practical sessions, meticulous planning, reporting and criticised conclusions. We had opted, most usefully, as it turned out, to follow the nursery/infant course, but many of us regretted our choice at some time during those years, for the early 1950s saw the height of the child-centred years, when it seemed that no young child could move or even draw breath without some underlying, psychological motive. Children were often viewed as case studies, devoid of their intrinsic humanity, so that those of us who had enrolled for teacher training as a result of our liking for children were, at times, in danger of losing our enthusiasm.

That last night there was no lack of enthusiasm. Lockers had been cleared, cases packed and, in some lucky cases, teaching positions secured. The fact that none of us had been officially notified that we had, indeed, passed the course was irrelevant, far from our jubilant minds. We danced, sang rugby songs and threw two years of work onto the flames, but that was because we were unaware of a vital assessment which had not yet taken place.

To ensure uniformity across the country, a random selection of work was called in, to be judged by outside agencies so that the internal marking could be balanced against the pervading norm. None of mine was part of this selection and anyway, being an inveterate hoarder, I had already packed my sweat-earned efforts ready for home. I only kept in touch with two other girls from the same course, so have wondered ever since about the future of the girls who had whirled, like Dervishes, around the destruction of their written efforts and who were then requested to produce work which had been confined to ashes.

Here I was, after two years of homesickness, two stone thinner and a large amount of debt to clear. I did not even know if I had been deemed as suitable for employment as a teacher, but then, on my first morning at home, a postcard arrived asking me to report for supply teaching at a local infant school. What joy! I was a real, grown-up, passed the course fledgling teacher.

Before college, I had had experience in schools, notably in special education, in a school where I was later to spend some of my happiest years, but my baptism of fire had been during one school practice. As a small operation caused me to miss the prescribed period in school, I was drafted later, all on my own, to one of the toughest parts of Bristol. Laden down with the equipment deemed necessary (by lecturers who had cars) I travelled across Bristol, on three different buses and arrived at the school gates exhausted. A large lady, clad in various flowing garments, emerged from the paint-peeling front door and drew me into the building, as if she feared that I would escape.

"Oh, I'm so glad you have come," she enthused as she literally dragged me towards a classroom from which chaos sounded.

"I've been desperate, trying to take three classes at a time. Still, needs must . . . I'll put a few extra in with you and then I can cope with the rest. Two staff off with nervous breakdowns . . ."

And with those few, reassuring words, she thrust me through

the door which she quickly shut behind me.

At this early juncture I learnt the inescapable truth that teaching is around ninety per cent acting and ten per cent know-how. I had already been given an invaluable piece of advice by my grandfather, a teacher of impeccable reputation and many years of experience untroubled by unruly pupil behaviour – "Start off as if contemplating murder and ease up gradually."

His advice that you are not there to make the children like you, but to teach them was somewhat contrary to the principles of the college, but I soon found out that unswerving discipline invariably brought a respect and liking in its wake.

Now, when faced with what appeared to be a room full of savages, I found my experience with amateur dramatics far superior to the psychological studies in which we had indulged. It was a case of survival of the fittest and I had to prove that I was the fittest to set the standards.

"Come on, girl, if you can survive this, you can survive anything," I told myself sternly.

I did survive that school practice and I have never come across such a tough challenge again.

I loved returning home and was determined not to give up hope of a local job until forced to look further afield. I scoured the evening paper regularly and spotted an advertisement for an assistant teacher at the primary school in Dymock. My application was answered immediately with an interview booked for the next day. There was no bus to get me there on time, but a friend's offer, to take me there on the back of his motorbike, was gratefully accepted. I did not have a presentable coat, so borrowed one of my sister's. My sister being quite a bit taller than I, it was necessary to hitch it up and fasten the belt as tightly as possible. This gave me an enhanced bust, but endangered my ability to breathe deeply. Gathering up the fashionably full skirt into a bundle before me, we roared off, the bike spluttering oil drops which I hoped would not land on my person. Wishing to make a dignified entry at my interview, I dismounted out of sight of the school, rearranged the excessive length of coat and walked the rest of the way, my friend promising to wait for me with comfort or congratulations, whichever became appropriate.

Ann Cam is a Church of England school, but I was relying heavily on having won the Ackland Divinity prize at college. I hoped that the acquisition of such moment would override the failure in religious knowledge which lurked amongst my scholastic achievements.

The school was built in 1825 and had originally included the headmaster's accommodation. The building was now totally taken over as school premises, with two long rooms either side and the centre space divided, with wood and glass panelling, into two other classrooms.

After an interview, which was not as terrifying as I had feared, the Chairman of the Governors, Canon Gethyn Jones, offered me the post of assistant teacher. I would have to board in the village during the week, as the first bus in the morning arrived outside the school at five to nine and the headmaster insisted on his staff being on the premises at ten to nine. He was perfectly entitled to do so, but those five minutes meant living away from home and paying in rent what could have helped to pay off some of my debts.

The 'digs' allotted to me and to the other assistant teacher was at the home of the village postman and his wife. We slept on billowing feather mattresses and stretched our toes down to stone hot-water bottles, wrapped in flannel, on cold winter nights while owls called to the moon from surrounding trees and gateposts. Dark evenings were spent by the gentle glow of oil lamps and candlelight guided us up the narrow stairs

Nothing can compare to the smell of an autumn morning in Gloucestershire. The walk to school was scented with elderberries and the tang of hips and haws. Those days rivalled the Spring when we walked past fields yellow with the famous Dymock daffodils and took the children through the churchyard, golden with blooms, for the annual Spring church service.

One chilly morning we saw a cow give birth to her calf on the verge beside the road, as the herd were making their way to a fresh field. In the evenings, little owls sat, like notes of music, on the telephone wires along the Ledbury Road.

The school building was overcrowded to the point where the slenderness of the applicant would be a definite advantage when applying for a job there. My class was in the smaller portion of the divided middle section, while the thirty-four children accommodated were about double the number who would have been comfortable there.

On the first day of term, my first in front of my very own class, the headmaster stood beside me and announced, "This is Miss Hauting. She is your new teacher," and thirty-four new-term, scrubbed clean faces regarded me solemnly. He then pointed out each child, by name, coming last to a pretty, dark-haired little girl, ominously informing me, "And this is my own daughter. I shall judge your prowess as a teacher by her personal progress."

In my innocent newness, I viewed headmasters as close to God in their wisdom and solemnity. I was not aware that they were capable of making jokes, so I was relieved that said daughter was willing and bright. She did not let me down.

Shortly after my arrival, the coronation of a new queen prompted the adventurous idea that the whole school should make a trip to London, to see the street decorations. It was extra-brave to invite parents to accompany us, as more forethought would have made us realise that mothers relishing a trip to London would, of necessity, bring younger preschool offspring, even babies. Amongst those, as well as grandparents, uncles and aunts, were individuals whose most adventurous excursions to date stretched only as far as Newent or, more daringly, Gloucester.

It was indeed a mixed conglomeration of generations and experience which boarded the London train, in the carriages specially reserved for us.

Arriving at the capital, lunches and teas already having been eaten, which is the usual, pre-ten-a.m. procedure on school outings, our motley country assortment set out on the next stage of our adventure.

Teachers and kitchen staff herded the children into and out of the Underground system, the headmaster playing the part of the Pied Piper. The number of extraneous children and adults seemed to vary continually, but those temporarily missing seemed miraculously to reappear at the next pause in our progress. The Mall was supposed to be our 'pièce de résistance', but, unfortunately, the gigantic poles which had held the angels aloft, had been removed, leaving enormous holes at the edge of the pavement. The holes, however, appeared to hold as much fascination for the children as the angels probably would have, but caused my heart to miss a few beats. I had placed George, a somewhat dreamy, biddable lad immediately in front of me, as he was sometimes a little vague as to where he was or where he was going. I kept a quarter of an eye on him all the time. He wandered happily along, amenable as usual, but suddenly he had disappeared. There, right in front of me was a space which had been occupied by George for the last two hours. As I went forwards, I found the next enormous hole contained a light brown head of hair, then an upturned face which said, "I'm sorry, Miss. I didn't look where I was going. You know what I'm like."

I thought of the line by Pope, "*Know then thyself . . .*" as I hauled George out, slightly muddy, but unhurt.

Much to our surprise, all those who had made the journey with us were on the platform at the appointed time, to make the happy but tired journey back to Dymock that evening.

This was my first taste of the unpredictability of school outings, but many more, through the years, were to be sources of anxiety at the time, but humour when viewed from a relieved distance.

CURRICULUM SANS VITAE

It's Standardised Attainment Tests!
I do the ticks, you do the rest,
And all of you are going to play
At silly things, day after day.
    I would say "Write it in your books,"
    But yet again, afraid it looks
    As if there's no more money there,
    For all the cupboard shelves are bare.
How could you, Tommy? Put that down.
It's not intended you should drown
The hamster. No, just make a boat.
The question asks you, "What will float?"
    Oh, Jane, dear, do please have a care
    Behind the door while measuring there,
    In case someone comes rushing through –
    Too late – I thought that's what *he'd* do.
William, that block's for weighing, dear.
Please, none of that behaviour here.
There's nothing worse than squashy toes.
Oh, Angela, do blow your nose.
    Now, while you're counting out the bricks,
    I'll just fill in a few more ticks,
    So when the Open Evening comes
    They'll serve to entertain your Mums.
It's whose turn at the water tray?
Whose turn is it to see today
If green or yellow, red or blue
Can fill up any other two?

Yours, is it, Luke? I thought it may
Be yours again, like yesterday.
It's no good telling me it's rain
When we're all flooded out again.
Where has the spirit level gone?
You're looking guilty, little Ron.
You hit the bubble with a clout?
Where is it now? You let it out!
  No, it's not funny, girls and boys;
  These are not expensive toys.
  They are activities designed
  To educate the childish mind.
Is that the bell? Thank God. At last!
I wish **I** could go home that fast.
Tomorrow's outing, on the bus . . . .
We'll need – a whistle, sticky labels, first-aid kit, toilet rolls,
paper towels, sawdust, the sick bucket – and lots of spare pants!

"MISS, THERE'S A RAT BEHIND YOU"

In the 1950s, Church of England schools were still tied to the PNEU system. This meant that, at a certain time of any prescribed day, teachers of a particular age group would be expected to teach round the contents of a stated page of a required book. This was not as limiting as it first appears to be and it certainly had its advantages, for in our country school in Dymock, where the number of summer pupils shot up during the fruit picking season, transfers between schools were made easier for children who had followed this set programme.

We were (even then) desperately short of resources and sticking to the prescribed system required a good deal of ingenuity. Children had to share two, three or even four to a textbook. Hands would shoot up to impart the news that "Page fifty-two's not in our book, Miss." Sometimes the said page would be found, having become detached and migrated to a new position amongst its largely loose-leaved book It took me a long time to realise that if missing pages were noted on the cover of each book, some of the chaos could be prevented. I could have copied the required information onto the blackboard, doing away with the tattered remains of books altogether, but the blackboard rested on a decidedly insubstantial easel which had to be squeezed into the small space at the front of the room. This prevented access to opposite sides of the room apart from a mountaineering traverse across desks. Several times, a member of the top class, on his way to collect dinner numbers, opened the dividing door with a flourish, toppling the precariously balanced board and endangering the number of pupils on role due to decapitation. In time, two of the boys, at the front of my class, became quite adept at leaping to support the blackboard as the dividing door opened, earning them quite a few reward stars for effort.

Some war-time shortages still persisted. Pencils were in such short supply that they hardly allowed for writing at the business end, let alone being nibbled from the other. Painting paper was non-existent, but decorators were generous with their old sample books which were our source of material for drawing, painting, shopping-list covers for Mother's Day and, of course, the inevitable calendars for Christmas. My family took very seriously the request that they think very carefully before throwing anything away and the children and I grew quite inventive about uses to which so-called junk could be put.

At the front of the room was a large black stove, a voracious gobbler of coke. The mantlepiece above it was a convenient place to warm the children's small bottles of milk on cold mornings, while on the huge fireguard coats and hats steamed dry. In the winter, some of the smaller children needed to thaw out by the warm stove, for we had a large catchment area and not all the children were on one of the school bus routes. Those were the days before children were ferried to school by car; noxious, chugging tractor, perhaps, but never a car. Some of the little ones, as young as four or five, made their way over the fields for several miles, whatever the weather.

During infrequent, quiet periods, as I sat at the old-fashioned raised desk, which perched like a raised guardhouse and gave an almost aerial view of my domain, I wondered at the random delineation of the concrete footing round the base of the stove, rather reminiscent of the Norwegian coastline. Patches seemed to have been added randomly and I idly wondered why. When I had been at Dymock for a few weeks, I set the children some writing work (not too long, having regard for the life of the pencils and the rarity of writing paper). As I drew my feet above the draught which, literally, whistled under the outside door, a shudder went round the room, then a murmur, out of which emerged cries of "Miss, there's a rat behind you."

Feeling proud of my sangfroid at what was, obviously, a joke, I told the children to be quiet and to get on with their work. For a few minutes, silence reigned, then a small gruff voice said, "Miss, quick, it's true – and they eats 'umans if they gets a chance." A lively discussion on this exciting possibility broke out during which I stole an unbelieving glance behind me. About two feet away was an evil-looking creature, sitting up on its hind legs, fixing me with a speculative stare.

I had only ever seen rats at a distance before and that in the open air. I was petrified and an instinctive aversion to vermin made my flesh crawl, but the children took it as a normal part of school to have rats popping up through the floorboards and they were quick to inform me of the comforting remedy.

"We all stamps on the floor, Miss. Then they all goes back down their holes."

The situation did not place the correction of their grammar at the top of my priorities, so, taking the chance that the rat would remember its route, we all stamped to send it back down.

The rat disappeared and I was advised to tell the headmaster of the visitation so that council workers could extend the concrete border round the stove to block up the newly gnawed hole.

The deputy head had coped with the rat problem his own way. The floor of his classroom was a patchwork of wood, shiny metal and pieces advertising engine oil and patent remedies. He saved all the tins he could get his hands on, flattened them and, together with metal hoardings begged from the local garage, nailed patches over new rat holes as they appeared. To cross his room was a hazardous business, tripping over curled edges of tin and hoping that the current patch, bearing one's weight, would prevent one's descent down a rat hole.

Despite the crumbling state of the interior of the building, the school was greatly loved and appreciated by the whole area. Not only parents of the current children had attended the school, but many grandparents and great-grandparents. The school was theirs, they were inordinately proud of it and supported all the school events to the best of their ability, but the staff and children of Ann Cam school must have been very relieved to move into a beautiful new, vermin-free building in 1974, leaving the old building to be de-ratted, refurbished and to be used for various purposes by the whole village.

Although a newly qualified teacher could glorify in the responsibility of actually being in charge of a class, there was another hurdle to be overcome before this status was granted permanence; a visit by one of Her Majesty's Inspectors of schools. We were used to having lecturers popping into our classrooms when, as students, every word or action could be criticised, approved or condemned, but a visit by an HMI could not be viewed as in the same category of experience. For one thing, there was the title; Her Majesty's. What officialdom that conjured up. The most important difference was that an adverse report from such an august body would negate the college's opinion that the probationer was fit to become a fully-fledged teacher. This fear was deeply embedded in all of us, although on reflection, no-one had ever actually heard of a probationer being failed on account of this official visit which was required by law.

AN HMI CALLS

I was on playground duty when an extremely small car pulled up by the gate and an extremely large lady extricated herself, with the expected amount of difficulty. She was encased in tweed, an ominous sign that she was something official. Instead of entering the playground, she stood outside, watching the children – and me – until it was time for the end of playtime. As usual, a posse of little girls had hung around the teacher on duty, waiting to be accorded the honour of 'fetching the bell'. This favour was only out-pointed by the glory of being allowed to 'ring the bell'. Permission to perform either of these was sure to set a smug expression on a small face for quite some time. We could have used the whistles, to be found in each teacher's desk, but the rust and various remnants of what could not be identified on the mouthpieces rather negated that idea. Mine, lurking in my desk amongst the fluff and a conglomeration of articles, probably confiscated from pupils long gone, refused to rattle when shaken. I took this to mean that its pea, or whatever whistles were supposed to contain, was absent, rendering the whistle soundless. There was a remarkable absence of whistle blowing amongst the staff, so I imagined that these tools were all gummed up, rusted or pea-less. We all stuck to bell-ringing.

The sound of the first bell signified 'stand still'. On this occasion, a few embryo pugilists were so engrossed in the corner of the playground that their occupation took precedence over the request to stand still. It may have been because of my mounting nervousness in the presence of the tweed-clad lady, but even I was astounded at the volume of my loud command, "Stand still." As the echoes reverberated from the nearby walls, every pair of eyes swivelled towards me and all movement ceased. Then complete silence fell, before it was broken by a slow handclap from the lady in tweed. An awful suspicion descended upon me. Could this august person be . . . ?

The college course had been grossly overloaded with child psychology and the all-embracing need for self-expression. Teachers who shouted endangered the self-esteem of pupils!

"That's it," I thought. "I have intimidated the little darlings by shouting at them. I am responsible for repression and a lack of development. I shall be thrown out ignominiously."

I slunk back into the school and was only mildly comforted by the thought of supervising my favourite lesson. I took the girls from Mr Jenkins' class as well as my own, for sewing, while he took all the boys for art, for we were still in the era which considered some subjects more suitable for only one of the sexes.

I was proud of my little girls. Most of them had neatly finished the ubiquitous mat, embroidered on squared material and had now embarked on pincushions or pot holders. The latter were acceptable gifts for some of the mothers who still ironed clothes with flat irons heated over a stove. It was impossible to go round the closely packed room, so I had laid out the bags of sewing across the desks for the girls to get on with their work or to squeeze a way to my desk if they needed help.

As I let the line of girls into my room, I saw with dismay that the large, tweeded lady had ensconced herself right in the middle of the severely limited space. A giant oak in a tiny pasture.

The girls astounded me with their adaptability. Those whose desks were empty sat down and invited those from the occupied centre to join them. They tactfully passed work to the displaced persons on the outskirts, avoiding all unnecessary fuss. I could have hugged and kissed them all. Those who were desperate for help asked their more competent neighbours or, failing that, mountaineered across the back of the room and up the side.

It seemed to be the longest lesson I had ever taken, but when it eventually came to an end the headmaster sent me a message asking me to stay behind after school. I felt like a naughty schoolgirl again. I collected up the bags of sewing and stacked them in the cupboard.

As the sound of the children going homeward faded, I tried to keep myself busy, tidying desks and cupboards, refreshing the water in the many jars of bluebells which scented the room. Then I concentrated on refixing the posters round the room which led a perilous life in this overcrowded space. I already loved my job and felt that I was getting to know each child in my class. It would be a bitter blow, indeed, if I had failed the qualifying course. There would be the possibility of going back to college for another year, but another year without a salary was impossible. I had only just started paying off a sizeable debt.

At last, I was summoned to hear the verdict which could make or break my future. Much to my relief, the HMI, whose name I never recall hearing, found my teaching passable. However, she had one misgiving about the sewing the seven, eight and nine-year-old girls were happily performing.

"At their age, surely," she said, "they should be fraying pieces of material, to get used to the feel of fabric. It is too much to expect them to be able actually to *make* anything."

I have puzzled over this remark for many years, but have never followed the advice. I would not want to be guilty of encouraging arrested development.

The headmaster did pass on another of her observations. Only once before had she heard a voice with such a formidable volume. It was when she had visited Linden Road Boys' School, in Gloucester and one of the masters had completely disdained the use of a bell. He had no need. His voice was enough. It was Eric Keys and he was my grandfather.

OH, DON'T GO ON A DIET, DEAR

Oh, don't go on a diet, dear,
Please don't get any thinner.
Please don't neglect the calories
At breakfast, lunch and dinner.

Inspiring loads of confidence,
A figure quite substantial
Sends out impressions constantly
Of blessedness financial.

If bony things were nice to touch,
With talents so desirable,
We'd all embrace the forest trees
And lamp posts would be viable.

I'd hate to think of waking up
In close juxtaposition
To someone made of skin and bones
That smack of malnutrition.

So don't go on a diet, dear;
Stay cuddly but trim,
Or I shall lose my greatest thrill –
Beside you, I look slim.

THE GOOD OF THE COUNTRY

The local countryside, in the 1950s, contained many families which reared a 'house pig'. This was a brilliant way of making sure that nothing went to waste, from scraps left over at the human table to the windfall apples in the autumn orchards. Although I never witnessed it personally, I was told that the sight of an inebriated pig staggering drunkenly around the fields, having gorged itself on fermenting apples, was not uncommon. Perhaps the lingering flavour of the fruit rendered the addition of apple sauce to the ensuing pork unnecessary. Whether from historical habit in country areas or from more recent memories of wartime shortages, the 1950s saw many families rearing piglets through the stages of children's pets to children's breakfasts. This was and is the way of life in the country and far more realistic than that which we town-dwellers follow.

This aspect of country living tended to shock me at first. I had been brought up to view animals as illustrated by the likes of Beatrix Potter and writers of sugary nature stories, for there had been little opportunities to see the real, live things and television was still in its foetal stages; the raw nature of the life of animals, as hunters or prey or as potential human food never intruded into our 'towny' childhood existence. Nasty things did not happen to the little pink piggies, only the wicked wolf, long ago driven to extinction on our shores, met an untimely death. Brer Rabbit was an enchanting little bunny, not the potential content of a pie.

I had had experience of the latter's occasional fate while staying with my paternal grandparents at Great Rissington, for Granny Hauting, having been in service all her working life, was adept at all the household crafts, not least making the most of every opportunity which nature presented. Thus, rabbit pie, cooked at the side of the black-leaded range, was a regular meal. Even as a very young child, I was only vaguely aware of man's inhumanity to animal as I was warned to extract the pieces of shot from the rabbit meat before swallowing it. That, and the distant sound of shots and the night-time squealing of rabbits caught by foxes formed a painful part of my education. Strangely, the huge portion of pig, dangling by its one leg from the large hook by the rear entrance to the house and from which my grandmother cut thick slices for breakfast, never registered as having been part of a living, breathing animal. Even the enormous joints of beef or ham, passed over the Home Farm wall each Friday, did not associate themselves with the animals to be seen in the fields all round the village. I had no problems with the Christmas geese. They were vicious creatures and they petrified me while they were alive. There was a certain vengeful joy in knowing that, as I unpacked the presents from Father Christmas, one of those fierce, terrifying birds was slowly roasting in the oven, in the stone-flagged kitchen downstairs.

Nothing had fully prepared me for what happened quite regularly at Dymock, though I must admit that my initial horror gradually, but very definitely turned to mouth-watering anticipation before very long. I came from a family of competent and occasionally excellent cooks, so the food at college had bordered on the repulsive, scarce as it was. I had lost almost two stone while training to be a teacher, but my first professional appointment certainly made up for previous culinary incapabilities.

It was customary for the schoolteachers who did not live in the village to board with Mr and Mrs Wetson. He was the village postman and could be relied upon for background information on all the families whose children we taught, making our job, as

28

'outsiders' more efficient, with a greater understanding of those in our care. Mrs Wetson cooked us miraculous breakfasts and high teas, considering that most food items were still rationed. The familiar rabbit made frequent appearances in pies and stews and vegetables were readily available locally, so Beryl and I were adequately catered for at the digs. However, the school dinners were a feature which would send Jamie Oliver into transports of delight. Before or since, I have rarely tasted food like it.

Everything was as fresh as it is possible to be before it entered the oven or the cooking pot, which is why I was forced, though not reluctantly, to adopt the sensible view of the countryside. Little pink piggies were not salient animals who could build their own houses to varying specifications and then outwit the Big Bad Wolf. On the contrary, they grew into large, lumbering creatures, frequently covered in mud, often smelly and, eventually, totally delicious. When pork was on the school dinner menu for the following day, the cook would mount the incline at the side of the playground so that she could converse with the butcher next door. As was usual at that time, the local butcher was also the slaughterer.

Most animals, shortly destined for human food, had no time to get stressed; they were never transported on long journeys or poked with sharp sticks at markets, but afforded a quick, unsuspecting death of which many human beings would be envious. Still, it was hard to keep this in the forefront of the mind when a request for "a nice couple of legs of pork," was followed by porcine squeals as the animal was secured. I was assured, by the children that, "They don't feel nothing, Miss. They's stunned first. You should go and watch, if you don't believe it."

I declined to take up the invitation and did my best to believe their assurances on the pigs' behalf. I am ashamed to say that all my inhibitions, concerns for fellow creatures and even the memory of the squealing vanished at the first taste of the next day's dinner.

It was rare for the cook to have to buy vegetables or fruit. During many a playtime duty I have had to clear an area for the landing site of vegetable missiles launched from a farm trailer, "For the kiddies' dinner, Miss." Cabbages and cauliflowers, still bleeding from their recent cuts from the soil; carrots, parsnips, swedes, potatoes, cooking and eating apples, plums and pears in their season all arrived thus, mostly by air, but some in heavy bags which the boys vied to transport into the school kitchen.

It came as no surprise when, after the first heavy snowfall, all the children, even the youngest, barely five years old, struggled through the deep drifts across the fields, their main concern being that they would be late for school. Some lucky ones arrived on flatbed tractor trailers, bouncing along the edges, in imminent danger of falling off. I don't think any of them did and even if that did happen, the snow at the sides of the largely deserted roads was soft and thick to receive their rotund little bodies wrapped in coats, boots, scarves and gloves. That rich, country fare bred them tough.

The fabulous cook, cherry-cheeked kitchen staff and all the local farmers, caring for their school and their inheritance, their children, as they had done for generations, were eventually devastated by bureaucratic dictate. An official visit to the school's kitchens, an intrusive inspection of menus and a ludicrous, unnecessary evaluation of scientifically proven food values, vitamin requirements, balanced daily food intakes, etc. was taken, quite reasonably, as an intrusion into the cook's domain and a questioning of her expertise. The safety of the vegetable produce, given freely by local farmers was questioned and the obtaining of fresh meat set the inspector's mind aghast. Instead of taking the logical steps of assessment, officialdom stepped in. A glance at the registers would have shown how absences for sickness were rare; even half-days were not often taken for visits to a doctor or a dentist. The only significant lack of attendance was the result of a measles epidemic and the measles virus is hardly a respecter of a healthy, sturdy little body.

A short time after the official visit came an official directive. Meat and vegetables were all, in future, to be purchased from the recognised wholesaler in the district and no local produce could be accepted. Despite the only logical criticism being that the cook had grossly *underspent* on ingredients for many years, the cook and all her excellent staff resigned after struggling for a while under the new regime; the cook's last tearful remark was "I'm not staying here to cook that muck." A countrywoman, born, bred and practised.

LESSONS FOR THE TEACHER

As a comparatively new teacher I was quite glad of the structure provided by the PNEU system which was followed nationally by church schools at that time. It formed the pattern for curriculum planning, yet left the individual teacher largely free to make what he or she could of it. I have always felt that this was an ideal arrangement, as the teacher was free to employ the methods which worked best for him or her within a framework. It was also an advantage for children moving from school to school, as they received a certain continuity which minimised any regression.

At the Ann Cam School, there was a nucleus of children from local families, most of whom were involved in agriculture of some sort and whose ancestors had, in many cases, lived there for generations. Everyone seemed to know everyone else and could recite the breeding history of the human population as readily as that of the animal holdings. It was, truly, a village way of life, with some of the older residents never having ventured beyond Gloucester in the whole of their lives. Yet they were content. The countryside held all that they desired and the rhythm of nature was the overriding music of their lives. Many times, I was astounded at their common sense and the deep philosophies they devised and understood. Coming from country stock myself, I have a great respect for 'earthy wisdom'.

Mixing with the indigenous population, in varying proportions, according to the season, were the travellers, some of whom had followed the same roads, at the same times of year, for generations. They came to this part of the West Country at fruit-picking time and, despite the absence of their children from the fields lowering their fund-raising ability, they mostly complied with the law and sent their offspring to the local schools. This was the first time that I had come across a phenomenon which had been described by my grandparents, both teachers, but discounted as folklore until now. My grandfather had regaled me with tales of the children who attended what was known as the 'Raggy School', off Lower Westgate Street, in Gloucester, who came from such wretchedly poor families that they often wore no shoes, yet were protected from the worst of the winter weather by being sewn into pieces of flannel for the season. Evidently, red flannel was the most prized for this purpose. Much as I had hated wearing a liberty bodice when I was very young, I comforted myself that at least I was not sewn into scratchy red flannel.

I never actually encountered the red flannel, but I came across several travellers' children who were sewn in for the winter. Strangely, they never looked (or smelled!) as if they were unwashed; on the contrary, they were invariably bright and eager to learn. The staff knew why the travellers' children pleaded to take home their reading books, for some of them had told us the reason. Every evening, the parents sat with them and wanted to have passed on what had been learnt at school that day. Although educational finances were so stretched, we felt that such far-reaching education was worth the wear and tear on the books and the occasional disappearance of a primer.

It was during this, my first professional job, that I had confirmed what I had long suspected; the teacher goes to school to learn, too. This was brought home to me most graphically when I spent more effort studying the prescribed curriculum than thinking about the little human beings in my class. Equipped with sets of large pictures, one of the fruits of a session with a persuasive salesman who targeted naive new teachers, I embarked on the required lesson for that particular morning. It is a truth proved many times over, that if the teacher is enthusiastic about a subject, the chance of the children being excited about it is greatly enhanced, so I approached the topic of the young of animals readily, with my huge pictures and plans for discussion. I hoped that this would lead to some lively writing about pets and other animals later. I chose first those animal babies that were familiar to me – puppies and kittens, then exhibited my other selection of pictures in no special order. Ducklings and goslings, foals and piglets went without a hitch.

The next picture was of a calf – not exactly the mud-spattered type one would encounter alive in the fields, but a fluffy, cuddly portrayal typical of my innocent, expensive outlay on 'Essential, Educational Aids'.

The class, all the members of which had been responding with enthusiasm to the previous pictures, suddenly went completely silent. The boys had been identifying the young animals with a disdainful tone to their voices, rather than be thought 'sloppy' and the girls were cooing sentimentally over the cuddly creatures and shuddering collectively over the less appealing ones, yet all responses abruptly ceased. I could not understand this unexpected silence. The only time I had known it happen previously was upon the unannounced entry of the head, yet there was no sign of the august figure now. It was a mystery how children, brought up in the country, many living on farms, did not know that the young of a cow is a calf. I suspected insubordination, how ignorant I was.

I asked several children, individually, what the creature in the picture was called, but only elicited the answer, "Don't know, Miss." The twins in my class were from the most noted farming family in the area. If anyone should know, they should, yet they both looked thoroughly puzzled. The girl just shook her head when I appealed to her, but the boy took pity on me. He walked right up close to the picture, peered at it for some time, shook his head, too, and went back to his desk. He was my last hope of salvaging my fast eroding authority, so I enquired, "Well?"

"Well," he repeated, "I *think* it's a Friesian calf, but it's a bit hard to tell, cos it isn't a very good picture, is it?"

With great relief, I agreed. I felt a bit of a fool, but was comforted by mentally putting the blame on the slick salesman of 'Educational Aids' and the publisher's artists who were, obviously, totally incompetent.

I had never seen such a satisfying lump of chalk as I found in the 'sports cupboard' amongst the flattened footballs, odd cricket stumps, 'daps' of various sizes (no actual pairs ever came to light) and team bands in a selection of fading colours and decrepitude. A more experienced teacher would have had more regard for the decrepitude of the surface of the playground, but I naively leapt upon the huge lump of chalk, thinking, "Surely, this can form the basis of a lively outdoor occupation, such as will be the nucleus of a satisfactory report on PE (outdoor) which I shall write up tonight."

Most of the children had their own gym shoes, but those without such home-bagged luxuries had to delve into the murky depths of the 'sports cupboard' to find two shoes which more or less fitted their feet. Lucky the child who not only found two of the appropriate size, but a left paired with a right. The really fortunate ones found elasticated daps, as laces for the others were in sadly short supply. The children hardly let a birthday or Christmas go by without making a plea for their own, personal daps, so although Health and Safety would have had a few strict words to say about the communal provision of footwear at the time, it did spur on local families to find the money for shoes for their children's PE, despite some of them having a struggle to afford the essentials of life.

The children being 'dapped' after a fashion and extraneous clothes discarded, we ventured out to the playground at the back of the school. I was to be grateful that I had not selected the front playground, as my exhibition was to be quite public enough with only the children as witnesses, without passing villagers forming a larger audience.

I intended a game of 'line tag' as a warm-up, so divided the class roughly into halves, each half at opposite sides of the playground. No-man's-land needed two parallel lines to be drawn across the space in the middle of the two lines. I hefted the satisfying great lump of chalk and found that it required both hands to control it sufficiently to make a discernible line over the decidedly uneven surface of the worn asphalt. Eager to learn a new game, the children watched excitedly as I stooped, moving backwards, with a wriggly line emerging from the chalk. Then my heel caught in a lurking pothole and I tipped, unladylike, onto my back with my legs in the air.

In that split second, I remembered all the old remonstrances about wearing clean, decent underwear in case of accident, but was overcome by laughter when I saw the look of complete horror on the children's faces. They had undoubtedly never witnessed a teacher on her back, laughing helplessly, but they gradually joined in and I heard from parents afterwards that I had executed a manoeuvre which their offspring would always remember. So a few ensuing bruises were, perhaps, worth a little lasting notoriety.

During the days of my grammar school holidays which did not coincide with those of the primary schools, and during the longer inter-term periods when I was at training college, I had spent as much time as I could at the special school in Archdeacon Street, not far from the cathedral in Gloucester. The building was that first used as the 'Raggy School', but now the lower floor was an infant School and the first floor of the lovely, solid structure was what was then classed as an ESN establishment (ESN standing for Educationally Subnormal). As there was no other provision for Special needs children, apart from those who were physically handicapped or 'delicate', those children at Archdeacon Special School tended to have greatly varying difficulties, some quite complex and to very diverse degrees.

The excellent headteacher was Miss Cleverly, whom I had known for some years as a fellow teacher at Sunday school and as a member of the thriving drama group to which we both belonged. I greatly appreciated her invitation to visit her school and it was this that had finally decided me to become a teacher. Throughout my training and my time at Dymock, I felt drawn to those children who found it difficult to learn in conventional ways and had delighted in devising methods of teaching that brought them success, so special education was already working its magnetic spell on me.

I was surprised one day to see Miss Cleverly appear, unannounced, at Dymock School. She was closeted with Mr Hobbs for some time and departed without coming to my classroom, but left the message that she would see me that weekend. It was an intriguing mystery, but I learnt later what steps had been necessary to accomplish Miss Cleverly's plan, although I still cannot imagine anyone ever having the courage to gainsay that formidable lady.

A vacancy had occurred suddenly amongst her staff and she was left with very little time to find a replacement. I was extremely flattered and excited to learn that she wanted me to join her staff.

She had managed to arrange a transfer for me, as both schools concerned came under the same LEA. This would leave Dymock with a correspondingly short period of time to find a replacement, but that could possibly be solved with a temporary teacher, something which is and always has been thoroughly unsatisfactory in special education where continuity is of the utmost importance.

So I had to say goodbye to the school where I had been happy and had always felt welcome, but that Christmas holiday was spent in great anticipation of my future, for I knew it would be exciting – but how exciting I was yet to find out.

THE HIGHWAYMAN

Highwayman Jake, for what he could take,
Rode forth on his sprightly grey mare.
Tho' the night was so cold, they both were quite bold,
A hard-hearted, villainous pair.
　　Jake charged down the road the Romans bestrode
　　When they marched up from old Glevum town.
　　To Cicester bound he covered the ground
　　As the fog and the mist settled down.
And then, through the night, there loomed into sight
A coach with its lamps all ablaze.
But the horses weren't able; they wanted their stable
And the coachman had seen better days.
　　Now who could believe that a maid so naive
　　Could be travelling forth in the night?
　　At only eighteen, voluptuous yet lean
　　She was a most beautiful sight.
At the sight of Jake's horse, the coach swerved from its course,
The coachman fell, dead as a stone.
The poor old man's heart led him to depart
Which left the young maid all alone.
　　We've all heard about the Highwayman's shout;
　　It's demanding your money or life,
　　But libidinous Jake, the reprobate rake
　　Put away his fierce gun and his knife.
He gazed up and down, from her feet to her crown
And his heart was as black as his hair.
Then, as he drew near, she trembled with fear;
Transfixed by his cold-blooded stare.

"Just let me approach and get in the coach,"
He said with a sadistic leer.
So the naive young maid, in no way afraid,
Said, "Do make me warm, I'm so cold in here."
I'm sorry to say, that by the next day
Her innocence lightly had flown
And very soon after, his demonic laughter
Accompanied the ex-maiden's moan.

Too wicked for heaven, the A417
Is their home, at the top of the hill.
If the moon is just right on a clear, starry night
The lovers are galloping still.
And so, at long last, as ages have passed,
Jake's hair is now peppered with grey.
He gets quite worn out with his wild, nightly bout,
So he sleeps well during the day.

So a rum or a gin at the Old Cotswold Inn
Or a snack or a dinner for two
Will make a nice break now that dissolute Jake
Has no energy left to mug you.

A SPECIAL INTRODUCTION

In the 1950s, Lower Westgate Street was much as it had been for very many decades. Grouped round the Cathedral Close, small streets, some of them no more than alleys, still retained the cosy atmosphere of an old, intimate town. Gloucester had originally developed within walls, which rendered its planning somewhat congested and new homes, over the centuries, had been built along the lines of those old, narrow streets.

Archdeacon School, with its red-brick facade and high, narrow windows, stood a tall two storeys, dwarfing the tiny, terraced houses around it. A tarmac playground, surrounded by iron railings which had survived the wartime appropriation of metals, was shared by the infant school which occupied the ground floor and the special school which was situated on the first floor. Across the playground was a rather bleak building, one end of which was used for school dinners and the other half for art-and-craft pursuits. The combined smell of long-cooked vegetables and wood glue sometimes overwhelmed both the appetite and the creative urge.

At the side, was a lean-to, where staff parked their various forms of transport and where children were strictly forbidden to venture – which was a bit awkward, as the front of the lean-to was open to the playground and just behind ad hoc football and cricket pitches. This rendered a large amount of time of the playground duty teacher supervising the under, over and behind search for recalcitrant balls which had, presumably innocently, strayed into the forbidden territory.

The special school took children in the junior age group, between the ages of seven and eleven. In most cases, infant schools of that era were expected to cope; no small achievement as infant classes then often consisted of around forty children. During the year before I went to college, I had been nursery assistant to my own, original first teacher at Calton Road Infant School, where the redoubtable Miss Morgan not only managed fifty 'rising fives' but gave us all a confident start to our school lives; something which many of us remember to this day with gratitude and affection.

By the time that I commenced teaching, the numbers game had eased a little, but infant teachers were still in the unenviable position of having overlarge classes, often without any classroom help, trained or otherwise. The more familiar I became with the problems of, and with, some of our Archdeacon intake, the more I admired the stamina and expertise of those infant teachers.

As I was to take the lower age group, the sevens and eights, I was allotted the biggest room which took up most of the one side of the top floor. The other classes were accommodated in two rooms opposite, while the staff and the head teacher's rooms were at the end. As well as the usual toilets and washing facilities for children and staff, there was also a bathroom. I was later to discover the undeniable necessity of the latter, when a coal haulier's son came under my care.

At first, being used to classroom doors which opened onto the countryside, the high windows which precluded any glimpse of the outside world, induced feelings of claustrophobia, but later, when it became obvious that the school was like an extended family making up a mutual supportive unit, there was no thought of needing the outside world to intrude on our everyday activities.

In a sense, special education has to create a world of its own, providing for each child what has been lacking, or giving support and shelter from often traumatic experiences which may have left a lasting effect upon the child. The 'three Rs' are always important, as they fit an individual to achieve a degree of success in life, but a frightened, traumatised child is incapable of meaningful academic learning and many children accepted into Archdeacon Street had far more severe handicaps than a lack of literacy. A teacher has to learn as he or she goes along, for theory is useless when it comes to general conclusions; this is a little human being in front of you, a unique being with unique problems. I soon learnt that firmness and understanding were to be employed as necessary; constant firmness in general and awareness of each child's potential and limitations as appropriate.

The confidence of all the staff was boosted by the leadership of Miss Cleverly. She was a wonderful inspiration to us and to the children. She never missed an opportunity to praise and encourage and her criticisms were always fair. What is more, the teachers knew that whatever we were asked to do, Miss Cleverly could probably do it better.

I have never taught in another school which contained so much humour and which brought so much innocent joy into the lives of children who, frequently, had never before experienced such a thing. April Fool's Day came in my first term. One of the staff – probably Miss Cleverly – thought it would be a good idea to play a trick on the whole school, but how? It was essential for some of our children to learn that having fun was possible and, harder to understand, one could be the subject of a joke without feeling insulted or hurt.

April 1st was bright and warm. Some of the biggest children were dispatched to the playground with instructions to set out the PE benches in front of the wall, and mats before them. All the children were informed that the school photographer was coming and that they should all group themselves nicely and each try to look as tidy as possible. The fact that no teachers were, apparently, supervising them, should have made them suspicious, but they were all so busy measuring themselves against each other and sorting themselves into serried ranks on the benches and mats, not to mention the frantic hair slicking and smile fixing, that it was some time before the flurry became an ordered grouping and we were proud to see how over fifty children, each with his or her difficulties, had managed themselves. The deputy head had been close all the time, hidden behind the outside door, in case of insurrection, but he was not needed.

It was a memorable moment when, leaning out of the upstairs window of the staff toilets, we shouted "April Fools!" Some of the children fell about, laughing, others had to have the significance explained to them by their more astute companions, but some formed a vanguard, closely followed by the main body, into the school and up the stairs. Luckily, the deputy head was fleet of foot and managed to join us, behind a locked door, before the indignant crowd got upstairs. The staff shouted their regrets at having tricked them. The children were surprisingly quick to forgive us and the general feeling was that anything which took them away from schoolwork was OK by them. It was fun and there were lessons learnt that day that would be much longer lasting than the lost hour of maths, English or spelling.

Dealing with the 'raw recruits', some of those who entered my class had profound difficulties not necessarily with schoolwork, but in their behaviour. We had psychologists' and previous teachers' reports, but those were often written by overstretched individuals within a limited time frame. Teachers, however experienced, could not be expected to observe constantly the behaviour of one child when there were so many others who may have had difficulties of some kind all within a class which needed teaching.

The first section of the report always contained any medical aspects, some of them quite distressing. The worst of these cases was a charming young boy with a great sense of humour who was frequently prevented from smiling, for if he did, his lips cracked and bled. He often had large blisters on various parts of his body, for he could not go out in the sunlight; even in a bright, sunless day he had to stay indoors, but the worst hurdle for him was the short morning journey from taxi to school door and visa versa in the afternoon. However hot the weather became, he had to wear a broad-brimmed hat, with enveloping veil if the sun were out, long sleeves and gloves and, of course, long trousers. In a big school, where most children were sailing through their lives with little effort, Gary felt himself to be a total pariah, but at Archdeacon Street, he learnt that everyone around him had their own problems and, although his may have been obvious, a lot of the other children had as much, if not more, to cope with. After all, he was safe indoors and it was frequently the case that some children felt safe nowhere. Gary gradually blossomed as he became accepted and we all missed his happy personality when he left.

It was quite understandable that some parents, hearing the words special education tended to panic, despite them usually being the prime activators in securing an education more suitable for their child than the one they could receive in a regular school. However, I cannot remember a single instance when a set of parents refused a place at that school for their child, once they had visited it. However, some parental visits contained conversations or created situations which, inevitably, have left a lasting source of great amusement.

One lady, loud-mouthed and 'blowsy', came to the school accompanied not only by the child at the centre of the situation, but a medley of grubby children of varying sizes, right down to the scrappy bundle she toted over one shoulder. One child of about two years old ran round the head's room, banging against the furniture and dodging mother's flying hand each time round as she made an obviously habitual, but half-hearted, attempt to discipline him. At last, the boy, probably from sheer exhaustion, stopped gyrating and stood still in front of the imposing desk. There was an ominous pause, while the child fixed an impenetrable gaze upon his brother's future headmistress. Then his mother showed the first piece of real interest she had exhibited since entering the school.

"Cor, look," she said. "He's pissed all over yer floor!"

The whole tribe was hastily accompanied off the premises before the perpetrator investigated the pleasure of jumping into the gradually spreading puddle on the polished oak flooring.

One fascinating sight that none of us could forget was the mother who arrived, again with offspring of graduated sizes and an obviously eclectic variety of fathering. A baby was almost smothered in her fur-collared coat. We watched, entranced, as the head lice ran to and fro, like demented ants, between the fur collar and the bouffant, matted hair, while their bearer seemed quite unaware of their presence. It made us itch for hours afterwards, just having seen it.

We did not necessarily have to meet the parents to feel amusement. I wished I could have kept the memorable note which accompanied a child on her first day back at school after some days absence, but it ran, "'Er 'adn't been, so I give 'er sumfink and now 'er as been so 'er can come agin." A child's internal workings neatly and succinctly summed up.

Many parents, although initially antagonistic to the whole idea of their child being selected for special education, became great champions of the school and some expressed their gratitude in overwhelming ways, but rich or poor, educated or otherwise, they invariably became our friends and were eager to reinforce what we were trying to do for the good of the children.

FOOD CHAIN

"I hope," said the worm to the tiddler, "that I'm not your dinner
today.
I'm not very fat and substantial – just look for a much bigger
prey."

But the tiddler, consumed with his hunger, took hold of the
worm, gave a tug,
Then swam on his way, quite triumphant, with an ugly grimace
on his mug.

A lurking great plaice, lying smugly and motionless on the
seabed
Sprang to life when he spotted the tiddler and swallowed him
whole, tail to head.

Above them a huge, looming shadow betokened a boat going by
With nets hanging hopefully rearwards that chequered the view
of the sky.

"I hope we gets more luck than last time," said Gregory,
stroking his pate.
"My beer money's fast disappearing. I'll never get drunk at this
rate."

They tugged the nets inwards and upwards – and flopping
around in the keep
Was the plaice wot had lately been feeding on the tiddler plus
worm in the deep.

So, as you sit down to your dinner, don't think of this tale or
you'll squirm,
For dissecting the white plaice before you, you're really
consuming a worm.

WATER, WATER EVERYWHERE

The western part of Gloucester slopes gently down from the Cross, the ancient centre of the city, to the banks of the River Severn which is tidal, the height of its waters varying, therefore, not only with the amount of rainfall on its feeder area in the Welsh hills, but also with the state of the ocean tides. While these conditions give rise to some spectacular bores, waves of sometimes admirable proportions which regularly roar up the river, they also render those in the Lower Westgate area a little like King Canute. In the 1940s, the river burst its banks and crept up Westgate Street, causing a panic lest the muddy waters encroached upon the glorious cathedral. Planks, sandbags and anything else which would prevent the crypt being flooded, formed a barrier round the ancient building, while the local children ventured into the brown, congealing mess swirling across the main road, daring each other to let the water rise just that little bit further towards the top of their rubber boots. It took a long time and many heavy downpours for the greyish slime and the unpleasant smell to disappear after the water had subsided.

Subsequent floods have never been so spectacular but one year, during my time at Archdeacon Street, I cycled to school to find that the last few yards had to be taken at a rush, with feet held above the flooded road. Water was lapping at the edge of the pavement, trickling over it in threatening little runnels which the caretaker was frantically brushing back with his largest broom. A Welshman, he tackled the English river with as much determination as had his forebears making their stand behind Offa's Dyke against the English invaders.

Almost all the children arrived by coach or taxi, private cars then being the transport of the very few rich families, so Mr Brock was on the lookout for these vehicles approaching, lest their bow waves should cause a threat to *his* boilers which were situated below the school and which were a source of great pride to him. They were studied, tended, adjusted, and cosseted several times a day and, since he had been in charge of these monsters, he could proudly claim that no head, teacher or child had felt too hot or too cold, whatever challenge the weather threw at him.

If the sight of him brandishing his broom at every approaching vehicle had not been so comical, it would have smacked of great bravery in the face of a possibly overwhelming adversary – the Dunkirk spirit, indeed.

As each child alighted, he was lifted over the watery gap (much to his or her disappointment) and deposited in a dry playground, an island in the midst of a grimy ocean.

By playtime, the floods had receded and the next day the river had retreated to its allotted course, but the smell hung around for long enough for us to wonder if we would ever be rid of it.

Shortly after this inundation, the council brought forward their so-called 'slum clearance' scheme for the area. This involved uprooting several generations of old-established families from their cosy, terraced houses, many of which had been lovingly decorated and tended by the residents, to new council houses where conditions were no doubt more convenient and, perhaps, hygienic, but families were split up. A way of life which had survived for hundreds of years, with each generation passing on experiences and advice, was destroyed and we saw many tears as the furniture vans manoeuvred their way through the narrow streets.

One of the main problems of this regeneration was the existence of a burial ground, situated just opposite the school railings. If ever there was a case to be made for cremation it was the sight of ancient bones being thrown into great wooden boxes. It was some consolation to know that they were reinterred in the sacred ground of a more modern cemetery, but the memory haunts me still. Of course, the children delighted in the macabre sight, especially as the song, "Dem bones, dem bones, dem dry bones," was a current popular hit and the episode gave rise to several interesting projects, led by the children's observation.

The most lasting and, at the time unnerving of these offshoots was the determination of Matthew to use his outstanding talent for drawing to make a study of human anatomical bone structure. Matthew was an attractive-looking boy, large for his age, but with an extremely volatile temper, roused by his pronounced inability to make himself understood, verbally. When he first joined us, he was put into my class with his comparative age group. He had a reputation for being disruptive and, when roused, dangerous, so that the head kept an unobtrusive eye on him, for the protection of all others in my room – including me!

When I saw Matthew beginning to get stressed, I had an idea of how he felt, for I had had (and still do have, occasionally) difficulty in finding the words which express exactly what I mean. This boy's handicap was worse, for not only had he a vivid imagination which desperately needed some sort of outlet, but his inability to pronounce the words he had been seeking for made him rarely understood. However, he had a magical talent for drawing and it was through this medium that we could make contact when the spoken word failed. With an admirable speed, Matthew could draw his ideas, questions, answers and, frequently, his total rejections. With my much inferior talent, I could draw enough for us to have a pictorial conversation. He learnt to read, but could not pronounce the sentences. We adopted his method of checking and charting his achievement by him reading a few pages and, later, a book, then joining me at the large table and drawing the story in pictures. I was often amused to think how illustrations of a hunt, drawn on cave walls many hundreds of years ago, were now emulated by the recording of the understanding of modern words in a book. It seemed to send history backwards.

After the episode of the disinterment of bones, I was somewhat surprised that the event had not spurred Matthew into a spate of drawing. How wrong I was. After a few quiet days, he became agitated when the piece of paper he had requested was not big enough for his purposes. I stuck another piece to it, then another and another until he was satisfied. With it flapping behind him, he retreated to the far corner of the room and reverently laid it on the floor. By this time, there had built up a great demand for me to deal with the problems of the other children, so, as many teachers before me must have done, I thankfully forgot about a quiet Matthew, until I felt a hand running down my upper back, probing my spine. Dealing with children who have diverse personal problems does not leave time to wonder at an occasional touch, but gradually the probing became more insistent and verged on the embarrassing. I had to stop Matthew's growingly intimate excursions, without stifling something which had intrigued him for days in the planning and now obviously meant such a lot to him that he was totally intent on its completion. I had to see what he was drawing!

I hated to trick him, but when he grudgingly went out into the playground at playtime, I went to look at why Matthew had demanded such a big, long piece of paper and what had necessitated his investigations. There, life-size, was the drawing of an almost complete human skeleton, the skull, neck bones, most of the backbone and all the leg, foot, arm and finger bones. As far as I could tell, everything was to scale. I found a book with a picture of a skeleton to give to Matthew when he came back in after play, but he rejected this with a vicious scowl, so I knew better than to try persuasion. I knew that he would not be diverted from completing his picture, so I appealed amongst the boys for someone to be in Matthew's picture. A natural sloth took up the challenge as a welcome alternative to schoolwork and happily laid himself down as a living sacrifice to art. The resultant drawing was amazing and I was anxious to know how anatomically accurate Matthew's drawing was. My mother was, at the time, receptionist at a busy doctors' surgery. She took the carefully rolled-up diagram with her to get the experts' opinion. All the doctors to whom it was shown said that medical students would struggle to draw such an accurate and to-scale human skeleton. Praise indeed for a child of nine who could scarcely make himself understood verbally.

Several attempts were made to transfer Matthew to other classes, as he grew older, but they all failed. I did not mind keeping Matthew, as he became increasingly biddable so that by the time he had to leave us and join a secondary school, the only danger was that he could become too protective of me, a trait that had to be guarded against.

Our experience had shown that there was a way to make contact with Matthew and this was followed up in his secondary school, although we never obtained much feedback about him. Perhaps this was a good sign, an indication that he found it easier to conform and to use a little patience. Many years passed before I heard about him once he had left school. To my delight, but not my amazement, there was a one-man exhibition of Matthew's art, arranged by a perceptive social worker who had recognised his talent. By the time I heard of it, it was too late to go and see it, but I wrote, via social services, a letter to Matthew congratulating him and reminding him of some of the enjoyable things which had happened while he was at Archdeacon School. I hope he got it and read it, but never really expected an answer, as he was not beside me to have our pictorial conversation.

The memory of some children will never fade from the memory of teachers. One of these was Graham, a sturdy, ginger-haired lad, with a seemingly unlimited amount of energy. He was never still and could eat a pencil from the top end faster that the rest of the combined school could wear theirs away from the business end. The continual supply of soggy wood never seemed to do him any harm, perhaps because it never got a chance to lodge peacefully anywhere on its downward journey. Graham was quite well behaved, while constantly guided into desirable activity, but anything static was anathema to him. Everything had to be big and physically demanding. He would write beautifully on a blackboard, but could not direct himself into the small movements required for the size of writing required for a book. He showed complete disregard for reading, for reading anything at all, until I made flash cards bearing active, or better still, athletic instructions.

It was quite exhausting just watching him, but it did lead to him drawing himself and labelling what he was doing, then being persuaded that if he graduated from the blackboard into a book or even a sheet of paper he could take his efforts home to show his parents.

If anyone really could have 'put a girdle round the earth in forty minutes' unaided by space transport, it would be Graham. He had a mercurial streak, but allied to unpredictability it could prove disastrous.

We had some visitors from Ghana, student teachers who were keen to enter special education when they returned to their own country. They accompanied us across the playground to the art room, where I did not fancy the demanding task, in the presence of visitors, of continuing with the woodwork we had half completed. I started dispensing paints and paper. Graham had other ideas. We had been making balsa-wood boats and he wanted to go on making his. He helped himself to a Stanley knife; that would have been safe enough, for all the children had been drilled in the right way to handle, put down and generally behave with such a potentially dangerous item. No child had ever cut themselves in all the years I had supervised the use of Stanley knives, but one of the overseas students thought he was being helpful, by attempting to snatch the knife away from Graham. He received a deep cut across his palm which bled profusely. The sight made him faint and the other student and I had a job getting him to the fresh air and sitting him on the step.

The shock had made the children momentarily quiet, so I left the uninjured student to restrain them, in one corner of the room, while I rushed across the playground for help. The welfare assistant came across immediately and arranged first aid until the shocked student could be attended to in hospital and I raced in to join the class. How he had managed it in such a short time, I shall never know, but in those few minutes Graham had almost totally covered himself in brown paint. He informed me that he was from Ghana, to which piece of information I could not think up an answer, so he just had to drip outside the art room until the welfare assistant was free to deposit him, and his clothes, in the school bath.

We always had spare sets of clothes, ready for such contingencies. Before each jumble sale, we sorted out clothes which were suitable for a child to be changed into and we needed as many as we could get, as they frequently failed to come back to us. However, they served the good of the children perhaps more than did the money we raised from the jumble sales.

There was one instance where patience did wear very thin. A beautiful child, with black eyes and dark, curly hair came to us from a temporary settlement the other side of Gloucester. The children of these peripatetic families were usually most rewarding to teach, as they were generally bright and eager to learn, making good progress in what was frequently a sadly short time with us. Looking at Donald, one would wonder that so much grime could stick to such a small person, but he was destined to be a reviled outcast while he smelt so badly. Our only recourse was to an immediate bath when he arrived at school and a complete set of clean clothes, for the ones he arrived in were rigid with unmentionable elements. For as long as we could, Donald was sent home in these clean clothes, with his home clothes in an airtight parcel. The clean clothes never came back again. Every morning poor little Donald arrived, on his own at the back of the bus, in the original, stinking garments. We tried 'forgetting' to send his smelly parcel home, but instead of forcing his family to dress him in what he had been given from school, he arrived in an assortment of equally filthy garments, more ill-fitting than ever.

The staff visited all the jumble sales we saw advertised, to buy clothes for Donald but it was disheartening to know that he would only luxuriate in each set for the one day before they were snatched from him, no doubt to be sold. Social services and the police were impotent, for any impending visits by authority seemed to be picked up by the antennae of this vagrant community so that there was never anyone around at an official visit, except, perhaps, a few menacing dogs. Donald moved on we knew not where but his joy at being clean, nicely dressed and, what is more, accepted, must have been a memory even more treasured by him than it was for us.

OUTINGS I HAVE KNOWN

During some evenings in the week, our building was used by a youth club. This was far from a satisfactory arrangement, as we frequently arrived on a school morning to find cupboards broken into and equipment missing. Far worse was the discovery of our children's work having been deliberately vandalised. Pieces on which our children had worked and which had given them, sometimes for the first time in their lives, a feeling of pride and achievement were often destroyed mindlessly.

Another almost weekly inheritance from the youth club was a broken window. This was annoying because of the shards of broken glass distributed across a classroom necessitating at least a day's disruption, which had an adverse effect on the children. The headmaster was, rightly, indignant that our hard work was so often negated and complained officially to the LEA.

The youth club was given notice that it would cease permission to use the premises if any more damage occurred The head conveyed this message to the whole school during assembly and threatened dire consequences if anyone in the school did damage to the building, so that we could prove that it was the evening users who broke windows, etc.

The two staff on playground duty that day were the headmaster and me. The bigger boys were given permission to get out the cricket equipment and, using rank, the headmaster demanded the right to bat first. It was a beautiful bowl and an even more beautiful bat which sent the ball soaring high into the air – and neatly through the centre of one of the upstairs windows. The crystalline crash was followed by the most profound silence I have ever experienced. By the time that the awed silence had turned to awed expressions (many of delight), the headmaster had disappeared into the building.

One of the boys had cause to thank him shortly after. We had the weekly use of the swimming baths in Gloucester. Two staff, of differing sexes, were required to accompany the boys and girls on the coach and to supervise the changing rooms. The attitude of the children to learning to swim varied greatly, which, with their lackadaisical approach to undressing, drying and dressing made the baths trip the least favourite occupation of the staff. However, the female staff were more fortunate than their male counterparts, for Malcolm moved like a human sloth. Sometimes, his movements were barely perceptible despite him amiably complying with a request. He got quite indignant when his speed was judged insufficient; he was working towards what you wanted him to do, wasn't he?

The head being on duty one particular swimming trip, Malcolm was set to start getting undressed on the coach, so that he had at least discarded his coat and jumper by the time they reached the baths. He was then chivvied into his bathing costume and joined the other non-swimmers at the shallow end. Two instructors took over, sensitively encouraging the most nervous children to enjoy the experience of being in the water.

Suddenly, the head threw off his shoes and, otherwise fully dressed, leapt into the deep end. He emerged, gasping, and dragged Malcolm onto the side where the boy emitted a lot of water, then asked, surprised, what the fuss was about. Surprisingly, the now shivering head managed to be quite restrained in his remonstrances, pointing out that Malcolm should not have ventured into the deep water. Malcolm listened, quietly, then, looking quite hurt, he said, "But sir, it's not *my* fault if they put too much water in the baths today!"

It was some time before the head could see anything funny about the episode.

The Folk Museum was quite near the school and was a great source of introductions to local history. Despite the stuffed cow, near the entrance, being so popular, it was possible after a time to get the children interested in other exhibits, especially when touching was allowed. With a special alertness regarding trapped fingers, etc., I always found a trip round the Folk Museum rewarding. The children never failed to come away with an interest in the history of their city and an awareness of how things changed with time. The boys were especially curious to see how the movable exhibits worked and to imagine themselves trapping or spearing fish in the nearby River Severn. This eagerness to emulate their ancestors could have its dangers, however. At the end of one particular trip, it being time to return to school, I managed to pry even the keenest away from favourite displays and line the children up just inside the exit. Despite what I thought of as an assiduous rounding-up, a count showed that there were two children missing. A pair had sneaked back and had to be found. An alarmed museum custodian was charged with minding the main group, while I set out to find the two playing AWOL. I arrived at the apple press just in time. One boy was gleefully winding the wooden screw which lowered the upper part of the press, while another was lying on the bottom layer, blissfully unaware of his imminent end. I have to admit here that my immediate instinct was to deposit both of them into the press before screwing it down, but professionalism is a binding responsibility, so they were grabbed firmly and taken downstairs to join the others. The relief on the custodian's face, at being relieved of his reluctant duties would have been comical, had I been in a more temperate mood.

Almost as close was our glorious cathedral. It is said that people living in a town or city often never visit their most beautiful and historic buildings, but I was born into a family where my father was an amateur archaeologist and a member

57

of the Glorious Glosters whose colours I remember seeing 'laid up' in the cathedral at the beginning of the last world war. My mother was a librarian and had assisted in the original sorting and cataloguing of the Gloucester Collection in the city library. It was natural, therefore, to introduce children to this richness around them, so I carefully prepared my class for a visit to the cathedral.

I pointed out that the building was as beautiful as men could make it, taking a long, long time over its construction, as it was God's house. We would be visitors and so would respect the peace and quiet that people liked around them when they wanted to talk to God or to listen to Him. As we walked past Bishop Hooper's monument, I only answered the question, "Who's that, then Miss?" but left out the description of the martyr's end, drawing the children's attention back to the solemnity and age of the cathedral, in front of us. They viewed the towering building with awe, their faces upturned, looking touchingly angelic, until Stephen asked, (innocently, I have to believe), "Cor, Miss. Is it even older than you?"

Professionalism, I reminded my mid-twenties self, as I calmed down.

The more artistic children were entranced with the patterns of light dancing on the stone floors as the sun shone through the glorious stained-glass windows and the lovely embossed carvings on the lofty ceilings and throughout the cloisters. The atmosphere of the place seemed to have cast a spell over these children with varied behaviour and learning difficulties. Without exception, they became calm and thoughtful, full of wonder.

They had been told about Edward II having been buried in Gloucester Cathedral after having been a prisoner in Berkeley Castle. I had managed to skate over the method of his death, so the viewing of his tomb did not evoke too gory a memory. The undoubted favourite item was the image of the son of William the Conqueror, Robert, Duke of Normandy. The children stood, entranced, at the portrayal of a knight in full armour, including his spurs, limbs crossed according to the number of pilgrimages to the Holy Land. He featured in most of the written reports of our trip, referred to as, "The chap with the daggers in his feet."

During this time, I became involved in several organisations which involved teachers and various aspects of education and so built up a circle of friends which lasts to this day. Inevitably, conversations between us often included the recounting of recent incidents which may have caused anxiety at the time, but which, viewed in hindsight, made a good story. One of these, concerning a school in one of the roughest areas of the city went thus:–

Two teachers having touched upon, with their respective classes, the days of trading under sail, organised a day trip to Bristol Docks. As usual, despite dire warnings to the contrary, many packed lunches had been consumed on the outward coach journey. This inevitably led to pleadings and threats to those with remaining food from those without, occasioning frequent tussles throughout the day. However, the day went as well as could be expected – perhaps better, as no-one actually fell, accidentally or by design, into the Bristol Basin – and the correct number of children appeared at the pickup point ready for the coach journey home. The exhausted teachers, anxious to consolidate their relief at what had been a successful, if traumatic day, told the children that remaining totally quiet for the first twenty miles would earn them the right to sing for the rest of the way back to the school. Some of the children seemed anxious to speak, but, after a final, assiduous counting of heads, the driver was instructed to make his way back to Gloucester along the A38, the M5 not yet having been built.

There was a persistent muttering from the children, punctuated by the occasional "Please, sir . . .", followed by reminders from the staff that permission to sing for the last stage of the journey was being imperilled by each utterance. At last, after repeated pleas for attention from a usually compliant boy, one of the teachers went to hear his complaint and was horrified to learn that the said boy had no idea of the identity of the child sitting next to him. The teacher had to confess that *he* did not know him, either. The driver was asked to stop, while the realisation spread that, not only had they kidnapped a strange child, but that one of their own must be left, goodness knows where and probably totally unsupervised. The guilt of the teachers was not eased by the many accusations of, "We tried to tell you, sir, but you kept telling us to shut up."

One of the teachers took charge of the 'stranger', alighted from the coach which was to continue the journey, and crossed over the main road to hitch-hike back to Bristol. A willing driver had taken them most of the way, when a small figure was seen thumbing a lift in the opposite direction. It was, indeed, the missing Gloucester pupil, so now there were three passengers for the accommodating car driver to deposit in Bristol where a distraught teacher was refusing to let his coach start homewards without one of his charges. The all-round relief can be imagined when the missing child was restored to him and the Gloucester teacher could, at last, return home – this time by service bus.

Thankfully, no child has been lost on any trip in which I was involved. We once lost the headmaster, but that was on another trip, at another school.

SUNSHINE

Don't argue with us, Sunshine. We saw you hanging round.
We saw you casing up the joint and sizing up the ground.

Don't make excuses, Sunshine. We know your sort of old;
We know of all the black sheep in this 'ere local fold.

Prepare yourself now, Sunshine, to come before The Beak.
It's no good grunting senselessly, you'll have to learn to speak.

It's useless swearing, Sunshine, or kicking them there tins.
We've seen it all before you – and sometimes much worse
    things.

Just listen to us, Sunshine. You'll likely take the rap
When dressing up in uniform of backward baseball cap.

Your droopy trousers, Sunshine, your razored, bristly head,
And misspelled blue graffiti on the Superintendent's shed

All weigh against you, Sunshine, especially when the hue
On your revolting trainers just matches up the blue.

Come with us, Little Sunshine, we'll make sure that your light
Gets 'idden quite successfully – starting from tonight.

NOT ALL LIGHTNESS AND JOY

Each of the children at that school had a problem regarding education. They had all gone through the process of being put forward by a previous school for consideration by an educational psychologist who had stated that a place within special education would be best in the child's interests and should be offered. Some had difficulties with learning which were quite severe at times, and the reasons varied.

There is, within the general population, a huge range of inherent capabilities, but, it was our job to teach independence and self-reliance up to the ability of each child under our care. This is the nature of special education and, with lower class sizes combined with the pressure of mainstream schooling taken away, each child was able to progress at his or her own maximum rate. In this, those who only needed a slower than normal rate of learning were, perhaps, the lucky ones, but for others whose difficulties stemmed from a chronic condition, educational progress was erratic and, sometimes, static for a while.

Without a doubt, the home background from which some of the children came rendered their management and teaching by far the most complicated and difficult. They had spent their first, most formative years in surroundings which had often given them no sense of right or wrong or even of belonging anywhere. Metaphorically speaking, they could be wandering in a vacuum, rootless, with nothing and no-one to guide them, no-one to foster a sense of appropriate behaviour or reaction to everyday situations. Their often limited ability to reason things out for themselves magnified the difficulties. As a staff, severally and together, we attempted to give them all a feeling of belonging and the knowledge to enable them to acquire this. In every subject and in all our activities, we tried to give each child a sense of self-worth and of a growing self-reliance.

Our school was a happy place, with very few disturbances to the quiet learning atmosphere necessary for the absorption of the 'three Rs' and an unfailing eagerness to take part in the more active elements of the curriculum. We watched, with interest and, we had to confess, not a little pride as children blossomed and became confident little people, but there were some things for which we could not prepare them to fight and against which we could not shield them. One of these was leukaemia.

Rosie was the closest to a fairy I have ever had in a class. She was very fair-haired, tiny and compact, with ethereal, pale eyes in a little, heart-shaped face. She walked lightly, as if her diminutive frame hardly sensed gravity. She was a compact little person, loved by everybody. The girls took her under their collective wing, treating her as the delicate doll she so closely resembled, while she received attention which almost amounted to idolatry from the boys. She inspired a huge amount of affection within anyone she met. She was an only child of somewhat elderly parents and had known nothing but a deep love all her short life in her home and now in her school.

Rosie was always ready for a cuddle, for she was an affectionate child. She was eager to please and tried her hardest to learn, in carefully graded stages, what was put before her.

Her developing physical weakness was almost imperceptible. Her daintiness had long been accepted as part of her and when this first turned to debility was hard to tell, but she gradually chose to sit on my lap for longer and longer periods, resting her blonde head on my shoulder and uttering a small sigh now and again. She did not feel unduly hot and sometimes appeared to have as much energy as ever, so we went ahead and included her in our plans for the visit to Chepstow Castle.

All the children were greatly looking forward to this outing, having tied their English, history, geography and maths lessons to the study of castles for weeks. Their playground activities allied to castles were not quite so acceptable, but still showed how the subject had taken hold of their imaginations.

As well as the other several helpers, my mother was to accompany us. She personified the universal mother figure, with small children being inevitably and immediately drawn to her, so it was natural for tiny Rosie to gravitate towards her as soon as she saw her on the coach. By this time, Rosie's physical weakness was becoming apparent and her mother, who had, naturally, been in denial of this fact, had eventually undertaken to seek medical opinion.

It was a lovely warm day when we visited Chepstow, with the general excitement quite obvious throughout a reasonably long day. Perhaps it was this contrast which has remained so clearly in my mind, for while whoops of joy and discovery echoed through the castle ruins, Rosie sat on the grassy bank, quite still, within my mother's arms. It was the last day she attended school; she desperately wanted to, but her body failed her.

As I watched her tiny coffin being lowered into the grave I knew that my sadness would be shared by all the children who had known her, even for such a short time. The memory of her gentleness stayed with us, as if we had been touched by an angel.

Very few children lived close to the school, the majority coming each morning by coach and, in a few cases, by taxi. Our consequential lack of contact with parents was a mixed blessing. It deprived the child of possible direct cooperation between home and school, although the educational psychologist made calls to homes and frequently ventured where no-one else dared. We were often grateful for his intervention, as he seemed able to calm a situation which could have become decidedly confrontational and was able to visit homes during the day which, of course, we were not.

One confrontation terrified me at the time. I was working late, upstairs in the old building and waiting for my husband to leave work and arrive to give me a lift home. I knew that there was reputed to be a ghostly haunting, but having never had evidence of the past headmaster who was rumoured to materialise occasionally, I was jolted towards belief when sounds emanated from downstairs, although it was not time for my husband to collect me. I froze as unfamiliar footsteps ascended the stone stairs and approached along the corridor. Through the open door staggered a short, thickset man, obviously under the influence of alcohol and clutching a green, glass bottle which he smashed on my desk as he came towards me. He was between me and the door and did not look the sort with which I would fancy my chances of survival if he determined otherwise.

As he came nearer, I recognised him as the father of one of our pupils who had visited the school when his son was due to join us. I remembered him as a jolly man, ludicrously protective of his large, blubbery wife, but his mien on this occasion was very different.

The building was solid, an edifice typical of the Edwardian quest for permanence. No-one would hear me if I screamed. No-one would be able to intervene in time, anyway, if this man took drunken action against me. The situation was frighteningly unpredictable – and I was totally alone in grasping for a solution.

Positions were in his favour; he was between me and the door. Strength was in his favour; he would have been able to fell me in one blow. I realised just the one thing in my favour, however. He had proved himself protective of and possibly a little in awe of his wife; while sober, that is. Perhaps that instinct remained despite his recent over-acquaintance with whatever the contents of the now jagged green bottle. As he reeled ever closer, it became the primitive situation of 'him or me'. Relying on the permanence of character supposed to be in all of us and not a little experience gained from stage drama, I relied on feminine whiles and any residual gallantry which may remain in this drunken man who was approaching with the sharp corners of a broken bottle trained towards my face.

I feigned helplessness and expressed a fear which was only too real, relying on the only solution I could devise. I lied. I told this comparative stranger how glad I was that he had arrived, as I had been terrified, being on my own (that had become very true) and now he had come to take me safely downstairs, where my husband would soon be waiting, if not already there. To my immeasurable relief, he slurringly assured me that I was now safe – with him to guard me – and that he would accompany me downstairs. Not bothering to collect coat or preparation materials for the next day, I did as this now solicitous man suggested and went thankfully down the stairs and into freedom. His chivalry did not extend to staying with me, however. Having elicited how tall my husband was, he disappeared.

It was stupid to stay on my own in the building and I never did it again, but the incident had rather long-reaching and embarrassing consequences. My assailant/saviour was an itinerant stevedore on Gloucester Docks who frequently accompanied barge loads down the canal to help unload cargoes. His son came to school by coach and was often almost smothered by stems, not bunches, but whole stems of bananas which had to be unloaded by several children, who hoisted the stems aloft and progressed down the gangway of the coach as a Roman testudo approaching an enemy stronghold, then, in a somewhat puzzled manner, announced that this was for Mrs Dowding. The huge bags of raw chocolate which followed were an equal embarrassment, for I travelled between home and school by bicycle; hardly suitable transport for such largesse. Having unloaded as many bananas or mysterious-looking brown lumps of chocolate as they would accept onto my colleagues, I gradually transported the remainder home slung either side of my handlebars or sticking out at a ludicrous angle from my saddlebag. My four-mile journeys home became quite a source of amusement on my regular route. It was all very embarrassing and there was also the possibility of being arrested for being the receiver of stolen goods, but the overwhelming gifts gradually stopped with the cessation of what I took to be the fuddled, guilty memory of a drunken man.

Sometimes, we had to deal with an aggressive parent and these were frequently difficult situations to diffuse, as resentment had often built up for a long time before the parent made the effort to approach the school. One father, who was employed on permanent shift work, seemed to be at a loss how to use his Monday mornings if he did not have to go to work that day. We dreaded his visits, as Monday mornings were usually our most stressed time, having to settle the children down again after what had influenced them, often adversely, during the weekends. His son was in my class, but the head almost always managed to interrupt his progress along the corridor before he could reach my classroom. One Monday, with the head otherwise engaged, the repetitive visitor had an altercation with some children outside the head's office, one of whom sensibly came to tell me that, "'E's 'ere again, Miss." I had had enough of these pointless disturbances and was not feeling particularly cooperative. By this time, I had enough experience to have acquired a little *savoir-faire* in the handling of disruptive parents; specifically, that the best form of defence is attack. I flung open my door, called to the familiar father and, as he approached me, said that I was glad that he had come to the school, as it saved me having to send him a letter asking him to come. I then added, in my best schoolmarmish voice (which I was speedily acquiring) that I wished to speak to him on some extremely serious matters. He was quite taken aback, which was fortunate, as I had no idea how to follow this up. He visibly shrank and became abjectly apologetic, expressing his regret that he had to come to the school, but that his son had forgotten his dinner money and he wanted to let us have it as soon as possible. It was my turn to shrink, but my surprise lasted long enough for me to grab the money, wish him good morning and disappear into my room again.

We often wondered what other interest he decided to follow on his leisurely Monday mornings, for we never saw him again.

REWARDS AND RETRIBUTION

Children came to Archdeacon Street School from all over the city, for it was then the only possible non-residential placement in this area for a child who was struggling academically, yet could be helped by specific teaching. In some cases the distance between home and school was an advantage for a child who had been so far brought up in a home where he had known nothing but neglect or physical and mental torment. I know that my journey to work aided my transformation from homemaker to empathetic teacher and visa versa in the evening; how much more may the time spent in the coach or taxi have given each child the chance to adjust to the very different spheres of his life.

By no means were all families disruptive and non-caring, but it has been a fact in every school in which I have taught – the parents with whom one would most like to associate, for the possible good of their offspring, are the ones whom one never encounters. They are absent from parent/teacher evenings, school sports days and fundraising events. They are like shadows behind excuse notes and enquiries about child absences from school, figuring in small confidences made by children about their home lives. I was constantly wishing that I could have time to visit these backgrounds, to be able to put each child within my care into some sort of home perspective, but this was an era before such innovations were deemed valuable, if not essential.

We did get visits from parents anxious to impart news of what was important to them, although at times we perceived no obvious direct connection with the progress of a child at school.

One family, whose antecedents had been known to my grandparents as pushers of wheeled barrows and whose journeys round the city had been accompanied by resounding shouts of, "Any old rags, bones?" had now made good – very good. There was one charming son, an amiable boy who was a joy to know, but who could only learn at his own, slow pace. It was rare to welcome both parents on a visit, but this couple stood out for their obvious prosperity. The father was dressed in a blue, pinstriped suit, checked shirt and a tie of alarming brilliance. The mother brought a piece of Africa to us, in leopard-skin coat and enough chunky jewellery to collapse a less substantial female. They arrived just as school was about to close at the end of the afternoon, but in time, they told us, to save their son going home by the usual taxi as they would be able to take him in the Bentley. The mother greeted her boy in a suffocating swirl of leopard and his father did what can only have been gleaned from Hollywood; gave him a punch to the shoulder which sent the boy reeling, but with a smile on his face which showed that he was used to this gesture as a sign of affection and approval. Up to now, there had been no obvious reason why we had been treated to this visit, but, family completed, we became a captive audience to a recital of the heights to which this family had risen. It all sounded marvellous to teachers struggling on small salaries, with large mortgages to pay and families to keep. The tales of trips to the racing venues of Europe and size of the risky bets (demonstrated by the spread of the father's pudgy, be-ringed fingers) were fascinating, but the last piece of one-upmanship had us all trying to suppress our smiles. Today marked a family quest to find a television with the largest manufactured screen, as they relished watching horse racing particularly and on their present television set, with a smallish screen, they could only see the centre of what was being transmitted, the main runners. They felt that they were missing out and were off to find a television set which would show them the whole racecourse all the time. The father informed us, proudly, "I can read tick-tack, you know. I shall be able to tell if them thieving local b----- is cheating me."

We still tend to feel that the size of one's television screen is the ultimate sign of one's prosperity and refusal to be deceived.

One family had kept us in business by producing a child each year, without fail. Every September, as the new registers were written out, the same surname appeared, followed by the bearer looking uncannily like his or her older sibling. As fast as the oldest one left us to go to secondary school, the next would enter our first class. Later that year, we would receive the news that another little addition had arrived and our hearts sank. We doubted whether the father had ever seen the inside of a workplace, his excuses for his daytime sedentary life varying from "Bad pains from me back" to "Just can't get up in the morning. Can't face the day."

The mother had never been able to cope efficiently yet the final sanction, children being taken into care, would have eaten up a large slice of council funds. By necessity, the children were attached to each other, caring for each young one as it came along and this gave the family a certain type of security, but it must have been an almost full-time job for a social worker to nurse this family along. We understood that various approaches had been made to try to limit the annual additions to this feckless family, but it was obvious that nothing had worked.

Then we had a radiant visit from the mother. Her joyful face shone out as a lighthouse amongst the seething mass of young children who clung to her skirts or sat, stickily, on the floor. It must have taken a huge effort for them all to be transported by bus to the centre of the city, then to have made their way all down the length of Westgate Street before climbing the stairs to the headmaster's room. I took up station behind the mob in case any made an escape towards the stone stairs. I was, therefore, and thankfully, out of the mother's sight when the impressive news hit the headmaster. Clutching a slithery baby to her, but otherwise unable to move, surrounded as she was by her annual yield, she said proudly, "We shan't be 'aving no more."

The head had his mouth open to impart his pleasure at this good news for all, but before he could utter his words of approval, she went on, "No, we've stopped now. We know what's been doing it. See, we 'ad a real 'ard mattress for all these years, but now the social 'ave got us a real soft 'un. So there won't be no more babbies."

It was probably the most restraint I have ever observed as the head's face registered none of the amusement he felt, but assumed a sympathetic expression as he told her, "I'm so glad. Now you will be able to give your existing children all your attention. Congratulations!"

Felicitations were indeed in order, as that tribe did not proliferate any more, but many were the conjectures about why not. Perhaps efficient birth control can be ascribed to the power of the mind. On the other hand, it could prove an effective selling point for soft mattresses.

Many of our children came from large families which had had support from close relations before so-called slums were cleared and extended families split up. Estates of identical flats or council houses sprang up, to accommodate families in 'healthy, spacious living spaces' and people were relocated to these according to size of 'unit required'. Young mothers suddenly lost the wisdom of their own mothers and grandmothers on whose experience they had relied when a child was ill, when a babysitter was needed or, essentially, they needed a few hours' relief from the gruelling task of bringing up children, for already there was a growing number of girls struggling with these tasks on their own.

Through sheer loneliness, some took in a man whom they thought would prove a companion for them and a substitute father for their children. Those who took this risky step while their long-time partners were in prison, bore the consequences when the sentence was finished. Many situations like this resulted in not only the girl being beaten up, but the children, too, although I was amused at being told a variation on this theme. Rosemarie had been taken into care in the past, for her own safety, when it was discovered by social services that her mother was frequently attacked by a drunken father. Recently, however, a more down-to-earth social worker had convinced Rosemarie's mother that she must stand up for herself, as she was a buxom lass and more than a match for her skinny partner, if she only had the courage.

As we were sewing together one afternoon, Rosemarie confided that her mother had 'won' the night before. The other children, standing around, were as curious as I was and just as amused when Rosemarie told us, "Our Mum said she'd had enough and if he came home drunk again, she'd give him a good going-over."

Several pairs of eyes went large and round at this prospect, as Rosemarie went on, "Our Mum knew what time the pub closed, so she waited behind the door, with the rolling pin."

"Cor!" the audience breathed.

"When our Dad opened the door, our Mum didn't half give him a bashing."

"Was 'e 'urt?" asked one of her transfixed audience.

"Not half. The neighbours called the cops, but they said it served him right and they didn't do nothing."

Reluctant to drop this interesting recital, the questions came:

"Well, where is he now?"

"Was there lots of blood?"

Rosemarie laughed as she told us that her father had disappeared and they didn't know where he was all night, but that morning his mother had come round to their house to say that 'her boy' had been very badly treated and that she was going to keep him at home with her, so that he wouldn't be hurt any more.

The general consensus of opinion was that Rosemarie and her mother were better off without him and that his mother was welcome to the wimp. A satisfactory conclusion, as far as they were concerned.

As a teacher, you know that there are children whose image will stay with you always. So it was with Pamela.

"Miss! Miss!" it seemed to be an almost constant accompaniment to any activity. Pamela was an unattractive-looking child. She had a moon face where the heightened pink patches were not in the conventional places, but sprouted randomly and sometimes in alarming lividity at various points on her face, neck, arms and legs. As if this were not enough to make one avert one's eyes, the candle drip of snot which permanently made its way, glacier-like, down her upper lip, completed a repulsive vision.

Because of her unwashed clothes on her grubby body, one could smell Pamela coming, hence most of the other children gave her a wide berth. She was obviously used to being ignored, as the solitude forced upon her did not seem to upset her.

Jumble sales are wonderful things. We collected several changes of clothes in Pamela's size, bathed her every morning and did our best to integrate her, but the upper lip problem did not go away. Now her "Miss! Miss!" was accompanied by a full-length swipe of her sleeve across the offending dribble. I can still see the sawing, sweeping motion in my mind's eye. The staff tried their best to make up for a mother whom we had never seen but who obviously did not care for her daughter and we fervently hoped that we had given her some sense that she did matter and that she did belong.

Recently, while meandering round a superstore in Gloucester, forty years were swept away when I heard a familiar "Miss! Miss!" There, sure enough, was Pamela, not only a presentable-looking woman, but with her nasal fluids obviously now under control.

At last, she was able to put her past fears into words. Belatedly, she told me that she had been systematically beaten by her mother and frequently locked out of the house, sometimes overnight. She had been constantly terrified, she told me, except when she was at school. She still recalled with unalloyed pleasure the strange feel of a bath of warm water and the delicious smell of soap.

"I longed for you to take me home with you. You were so kind to me," she said, at last. I had to invent an urgent appointment and leave her before my tears flowed. Again, I felt the huge responsibility of being a teacher and the immeasurable regret for not having seen the depths of Pamela's despair at the time.

Micky came from what would have been a large family, but it seemed to be a tribal custom that all children were shared out between the extended kin. This still left three siblings living with Micky's mother, which is as well, as she was totally amoral. She not only gave her children no moral guidance, but encouraged them to shoplift, especially for groceries, so that her social security money could be spent on alcohol and cigarettes. Perversely, she punished Micky if he ever stole anything for himself, although he must have been perpetually hungry.

We were aware that many of our children existed in such moral and financial poverty, so throughout the year, the staff dropped their sixpences into a special tin on the staffroom window sill. By the time that Christmas came round, there was a sizeable store to be dropped into the Christmas puddings, with a good proportion going to the poorest children while their attention was distracted. They would all have to be warned to eat their puddings carefully, as they never knew what they might find in them. All our collecting was worthwhile when we saw the looks of wonder on the faces of the children who had never had their own money obtained legally.

Special education was the first branch to be aware that the children involved needed more than understanding and sympathy. Standards at home were often of the poorest and many had quite lengthy journeys to school. There were several cases where lack of food at home could be traced, when children gradually became healthier, more alert and growing during term time, receiving big portions of good food each lunchtime. However, those same children returned to us, after holidays, wan and lethargic. We felt great concern that, even during terms, children were travelling to school for some time, often on cold mornings and with empty stomachs. The staff resolved that, if the local education authority approved, we would do something about that.

Our head put forward our proposals and they were accepted. Instead of the daily one-third of a pint of milk allotted to each child every day, there would be two-thirds, so that bowls of cereal could be provided at the start of each morning. We noticed a definite improvement in the alertness of the children, but were surprised to read, some time later in the local press, a letter from the chairman of the education authority bemoaning the need to feed children at school in the morning. She ended by writing that "teachers will be expected to kiss them all goodbye next".

We had been doing that for years!

DESIGNS AND DISAPPOINTMENTS

I had been married for over a year, yet several of the children were still confused. One boy, in particular, frequently followed me round the building or playground saying,

"You're *really* Miss Hauting, aren't you, Miss?"

The reassurance that I had only changed my name and status brought a knowing look to his face and the whispered rejoinder, "You're only *pretending* to be Mrs Dowding. I know. You're really Miss Hauting."

We lived in the same area, so for years it was necessary to dodge his notice, for if I did not I would hear his voice booming from the back of the bus or across the road, "You're *really* Miss Hauting. I know."

This confusion could have stemmed somewhat from how the news of my imminent wedding was told to the children at the last assembly before the Whitsun holiday. The headmaster announced that Miss Hauting would no longer be a teacher at the school, but that Mrs Dowding would take her place after the week's holiday. Children with any degree of autism took this literally and could not understand how two people could look the same, behave the same and appear to be identical in every way. They even wore each other's clothes! I was being watched with suspicion.

In a creepy sort of way, this strange concept followed me to my new home. A collection amongst the staff and children had enabled them to present the leaving Miss Hauting with a huge framed print of my favourite picture; *The Laughing Cavalier*, by Frans Hals. When I was a very little girl I had been fascinated by what I took to be a picture of my father, as it was so like him. I must have thought the fancy costume a possible variation on his Territorial Army dress uniform, yet after this misconception faded, I still harboured a faithful love for the picture.

As my only portrayal of the cavalier had been comparatively small, I resolved to put my new, big picture where he could be seen at his best. At the top of the stairs seemed to be a most advantageous spot, it was well-lit and showed up nicely against the pristine wall of our new house. Emerging naked from the bathroom after my first morning shower, the picture welcomed me with its long familiarity, but it was not long before only its familiarity remained. Big, brown, amused eyes followed every movement – embarrassing enough when I passed with bundles of clothes for the airing cupboard, but even more so when I passed with no clothes at all. I found myself scuttling across the landing and actually blushing, such was the power of those painted eyes. He had to go to a more impersonal stand, which is why, ever since, he has inhabited a sitting room where residents and visitors can be expected to remain fully dressed.

Not quite Frans Hals, but an accomplished artist, the deputy head was delighted when the infant school vacated the lower part of the building and we inherited both floors. He had long seen the featureless stairwell as a desert longing to be beautified. He spent many hours after school drawing the outlines for the older children to paint in blocks of colour. The project lasted for quite a few weeks, but the result was stunning. A beanstalk, with Jack having climbed halfway up, formed the connection to a fearsome giant at the top and an anxious mother and equally anxious-looking cow at the bottom. Little Red Riding Hood emerged from the woods surrounding them, with the wolf peering from behind the trees. Little Miss Muffet appeared, as yet unfazed by the huge black spider descending above her and on the top floor Humpty Dumpty sat grinning on his wall while the king's mounted men waited for the inevitable tumble.

The effect of this riot of colour and portrayal of the familiar had a positive effect on the staff as well as the children. How lucky we were to have amongst us a member of staff with such talent and an organisation which valued such things. Many of the children were inspired to paint and to invent their own designs after seeing what a difference a little ingenuity could make to all our lives.

That big, old building seemed to inspire the creation of colourful additions to every classroom and each teacher contributed in different ways. My youngest children gained confidence, perhaps for the first time, from seeing their work displayed on the wall, many being reluctant to take such things home. We knew why. There can be nothing so dispiriting for a small child as being pleased with an achievement which is then either ignored or even destroyed in front of them; better by far to have such work displayed on the classroom wall where its very presence bore witness to its worthiness.

Now that we had the whole building to ourselves, there was scope for so much more, especially space for activities to burn off excess energy during spells of inclement weather. The long corridors were ideal for staging tugs of war, relay races, paired activities which encouraged cooperation and agility competitions which taught the children that one often has to accept defeat.

If only I had followed that latter principal.

After days of rain and running out of innovative ideas, the headmaster decided on a high-jump competition. Those not wishing to compete or who failed the next height were arranged on both sides of the corridor and plenty of PE mats softened the landing of those attempting the championship. As is customary in most special schools, the staff joined in, but expected to be outclassed by the older children. Soon, I was the only member of staff left in the competition and maintain, as my excuse, that I carried the reputation of the teachers to remain in there, fighting for glory. As I arranged my skirt in an unladylike tucking, I ran up to the pole and vaulted over it, to resounding cheers, followed by what sounded like rain pattering throughout the corridor. My two-stranded necklace of round, white beads had exploded during my leap and were now pattering, as myriads of tiny mouse feet, in all directions. My exertions must have generated a huge impetus, as the beads kept bouncing for some minutes, despite the children's scramble to retrieve them. I gratefully received all rescued contributions and added them to the beads which had fallen inside my clothes but for days individuals were hailing me with, "Here's another one, Miss." Some of the older boys postulated, in loud voices, where the latest finds may have been held up, but I ignored them.

Records of scholastic progress had to be kept, of course, and it was important to incorporate award systems to keep the ambience positive. I incorporated the usual chart with stars for effort, making sure that each child was awarded according to their ability, not by comparison to the rest of the class, but the word-reading record was by far the most popular and, in some ways surprising. I made a high ladder for each of the reading books, with a word on each rung, starting at the bottom with the first new word encountered. Push-through paper clips provided secure positions for the little cardboard girl or boy made by each child, who wrote their name on the back, as for sportsmen. As the children opted to read the words they thought they knew, if successful, their boy or girl moved up the ladder. At the top, in a sky of brilliant blue, dotted with cotton-wool clouds, garishly wrapped chocolates were stuck like bizarre stars. These were awarded, according to choice, to anyone reaching such glorious heights. The eagerness with which the children sought to learn new words was wonderful, but what bordered on the miraculous was the way that only those reaching the top of each ladder acquired the envied sweets. None were ever stolen, which was most gratifying if not surprising, considering the background and past reputation of many of our children.

These little cardboard dolls gave rise to another idea. Another version of an alter ego climbing ladders could, perhaps, help with some of the problems experienced by our small charges. The need to be cuddled was often in evidence as was the need for instant attention, yet there were some who, although showing no other autistic tendencies, could not bear to be touched. We could not divine where some of these traits originated, but we could do our best to alleviate them. I accepted with gratitude any eminently cuddly toys and put them in a quiet corner where there were cushions and a stretch of carpet and was surprised at the use the children made of this area. Some just wanted a quiet, solitary interlude, others read to teddy or some other uncritical stuffed animal, some just fell asleep, but it was obvious that this corner and its contents fulfilled a need.

So it was combined with the climbing-doll idea. Two yards (then) of pinky/tan material, a good pair of cutting-out scissors, my mother's sewing machine and a half-term holiday resulted in various bag shapes for bodies, heads, arms and legs. Anyone willing was coerced into cutting up soft, clean rags into tiny pieces to provide material for stuffing.

The project took off with even more enthusiasm than I had hoped for. Little fingers were busily stuffing bodies, heads, arms and legs and then sewing them together. Every playtime and dinner time staff, dinner ladies, even the caretaker could be seen securing heads and limbs which had only been attached in an arbitrary way, sometimes in the wrong places. An HMI for Special Education came in during this time, but declined to help with the sewing, although he professed himself impressed with the whole idea and asked to be invited back when the dolls were finished. It may have been at his instigation that I appeared, surrounded by my little doll makers, on the cover of the next *Special Education* magazine, but had no opportunity to bask in fame, as there were demands for clothes for the dolls – not ordinary clothes, but, "Mine wants to be a cowboy, Miss" or "I want mine to be Frankenstein."

My time was now curtailed by the necessity to comfort Frank, a boy who exhibited an abnormal amount of resentment and viciousness, a result of overweening strictness and cruel punishment at home. Passing on his experiences, he had almost completed his doll when a sudden burst of viciousness overcame him. He ripped apart as much of his work as he could, then attacked the rest with scissors. Then he cried uncontrollably. As soon as he would let me, I held him tightly and waited until his sobs subsided. It was going to be difficult to put this right, but his stuttered remark helped.

"I'll bet you wouldn't have done that to *your* doll, would you, Miss?"

So I was able to tell him that I had completely forgotten to make a doll myself and I wished that I had so that I could see what it turned out like. I told him that I was a bit old for a doll and that I would be laughed at if I took one home, so I would be grateful if he would dress it and take it home with him. The joy on his tear-stained face sustained me all that evening and first part of the night while I cut out, assembled, stuffed and sewed together a replacement doll. This one Frank treated with gentleness and took home – "To keep locked up in me cupboard, Miss." I hoped it would give him something to cuddle and to comfort him for a long time.

I loved all those children who came into my care. I did not always like them, but time has confirmed my belief that, to deal with children, you must always feel love for them, for they will know. A dislike of their behaviour can be tolerated by them and by you, for that does not strike at the foundation of a loving relationship.

I was ecstatic, therefore, when the doctor who had attended my birth confirmed that I was to become a mother. I hugged the knowledge to myself, feeling the onset of broodiness that creeps up on many pregnant women, undertaking the sad task of giving in my notice to leave Archdeacon Street School with diminished regret because of my condition. This child would be the first grandchild on either side of the family and was being anticipated by so many people.

But it was not to be. I had a few more days to complete the term when a miscarriage ended the existence of a much wanted child and I was left with a feeling of loss and, for a time, a sense of total unfairness. I had given so much of myself to other people's children, yet was denied this one of my own. I was overcome with a deep sadness.

A HOUSE SLOB

Me bed is all unmade and rumpled, the bathroom is full up with
steam,

The towels are soggy and crumpled and the sink could do with
a clean.

I haven't washed up since me breakfast, the mugs and the
dishes just lurk.

The windows are letting some light in, despite being covered
in murk.

Me garage is cluttered with rubbish and leaves that blow in
through the door,

And the shelves became so overcrowded that things just end up
on the floor.

Me car is parked in there, somewhere; the poor thing could do
with a wash,

When I take it out, parked by a clean one, I'm ashamed that it
don't look too posh.

The sitting room's knee-deep in knitting, the table is covered
in books.

There is a clear path to the tele, but anyway, nobody looks.

But my garden – oh, yes, in my garden, the daffodils dance in
the wind

And the winter-flowering jasmine has the best scent that you'll
ever find.

Primroses exploding in sunshine make a pool of pale yellow
and green

With purple and white nodding crocus, forsythia and cowslips
between.

I can't whip up interest in housework, for dusting and cleaning's
not me,

But just let me out in the garden to wallow in nature – that's
me!

PLOUGHING A NEW FURROW

So, I watched as the bulbs burst forth from the earth, the trees became freshly clothed with delicate Spring leaves and experienced the balm of working in our newly cultivated garden. But all the while there was something missing, something which nagged away at the back of my mind, something which ought to be included in my life, but which was no longer there.

It was not just the loss of my own child which had created this gap, it was the lack of contact with the minds of children that I missed to an increasing degree. I think I missed the irreplaceable sense of achievement when a child discovers what is for them a revelation; a step towards realising that a share of the world is theirs.

The advertisement in the evening paper described a new type of post at a city school. It was for an entirely new type of job as a part-time (five hours a week) 'Teacher of Backward Readers', a term which, no doubt, would be couched in far more politically correct terms years later.

I could hardly wait for the school to be opened the following morning so that I could ring to enquire how to apply. After taking my name and a brief record of my experience, the secretary asked me to ring back later. When I did so, to my complete surprise, I was invited for an interview that afternoon. Luckily, the school was on the local bus route, so I arrived at St Peter's Junior School at the beginning of the afternoon session and was shown immediately into the headmaster's study. There, I was addressed as "My dear" by Mr Breen who made me feel quite at home with a cup of tea and his complete lack of formality. In my ignorance, I had not then realised that heads get together at meetings and, inevitably, discuss forthcoming vacancies and recommend suitable candidates to each other.

The post of 'Teacher of Backward Readers' was a new venture within the local authority. St Peter's was then the largest primary school in Gloucester, with children being bussed in from all areas to obtain a Roman Catholic education. The registers read like a list from the United Nations, a rare thing in those days, so it could be concluded that perhaps English would not be the tongue spoken in some homes. Mr Breen explained that many of their children came from undoubtedly caring families which, nonetheless, were often large and, in many cases, struggling financially. On the other hand, the cooperation of the parents was without equal, so that any effort put in by the school was always appreciated by the whole family.

All this was explained to me at great length and, at playtime, I was taken to the staffroom to be introduced to the staff, including two teaching sisters. Back in the head's study, I was offered the post, but warned that my appointment would have to be renewed by the Canon at the beginning of each term as, although I had been confirmed into the Church of England, I am not of the Roman Catholic faith. I understood that this was so that, if a suitable Roman Catholic teacher should apply for a post, he or she would be given preference, so that the ethos of the school should remain.

Confirmation of my appointment arrived by post a few days later and gave me a unique challenge. The position was an entirely new one; I did not have to follow anyone else's methods, had been allotted a certain amount of money for books and could arrange my own timetable according to the needs of the children and the willingness of the staff to release individuals from other lessons.

The front entrance to the school opened into an area called the 'crush hall' where I was to be stationed, with a cupboard for my educational equipment in the staffroom. The latter remained completely empty until the books I had ordered arrived. In the meantime, I had to test the reading age of any child, in any class, where the teacher felt there were difficulties in mechanical achievement or apparent understanding of the written word. These results were then to be set against the chronological age so that the discrepancy could be recorded – the 'Reading Quotient'. This enabled those most in need of remedial help to have some time allotted to them, with preference given to the younger age groups, hopefully to prevent consolidation of failure in future.

It was essential to test each child away from the rest, as an inability to read does not preclude the ability to memorise and repeat what has just been read by one's previous classmate. This short period of privacy with each child gave me just a taste of the individual attitudes – unfailingly polite – and a general feeling for the size and nature of the general problem. The latter was enormous, as I found out when I worked out the Reading Quotients. How was I ever going to spread my help most effectively over so many within just five hours a week?

As soon as Mr Breen saw the results of the tests, he put in a request for more hours to be allotted to my post, but financial restraint indefinitely delayed this coming to fruition. Meantime, I tried to arrange a timetable to suit everyone, a task which proved impossible, as some teachers refused to allow their children to miss any class lessons. I respected their reluctance to allow the missing of religious instruction; after all, that was the main reason the parents had chosen that school for their offspring, but surely, with remedial help for the most inept children, the job of each class teacher would be made a little easier. Mr Breen took it upon himself to solve the problem, which he did, by the expedient, I heard later, of arguing that an efficiently educated child would become a much more effective member of their religion and of society and would be better equipped to bring up the next generation.

My hours were to be spread over three mornings and each session would start with a group of the most backward children during the school assembly. Thereafter, groups of about eight would be allotted as much time as possible. It was tempting to increase the size of each group and therefore, the frequency of help, but oversized groups would defeat the object of specific, individual help.

At first, as could be expected, there developed a mild stigma to being in 'one of Mrs Dowding's groups', until it dawned on the majority that being in 'one of Mrs Dowding's groups' often released the happy escapee from some hated class chore. When the new books arrived, my 'chicks' proudly displayed them and that was the end of the stigma, but gave rise to the awkward situation of having to refuse a place to other children who professed their inability and came close to tearful begging for help. In some cases this was undoubtedly because my groups were seen as a welcome escape from the monotony of the classroom, but I witnessed obvious distress from frustrated, saddened children who were desperately aware that they needed help that, sadly, was not forthcoming.

As I grew in confidence and expertise, the games I made enabled the necessary catching-up to continue at home, where they were greatly appreciated and enjoyed by whole families. Each of these games was designed to meet the needs of a specific difficulty – sometimes of one, specific child, but because it is fun to play games, this method of teaching was most effective. What is more, the children were actually asking for more work and the teachers were beginning to allow their remedial activities to spill over into the classroom. This resulted in the learning from my games benefiting some of those for whom there was no room in my special groups.

It was a happy school, with respect for each other high on the list of requirements. I soon got used to being addressed as "madam", as the equivalent to "sir" for the male members of staff. Mr Breen led his team with a benign attitude which could become as firm as events dictated for the smooth running of his school. He encouraged innovation, as long as he had a chance to assess it before it was put into practice, and never omitted praise for work well done – by children or staff.

I welcomed the chance to act as supply teacher when a regular member of staff was absent; after all, a mortgage needs paying regularly, but when I became pregnant again, I took medical advice to curb my hours to remedial work and even to further restrict any physical efforts in the months leading up to the birth. I had been happy and made to feel welcome at St Peter's, but left with the satisfaction of knowing that any success I had achieved helped to resolve the LEA. shortly to install 'Teachers of Backward Readers' in several schools where there was the greatest need. I like to think that this saved some children from permanent despair.

In the autumn, I was blessed with a son and, sixteen months later, a brother for him. As many parents will have realised, your own children are the best toys you ever have and however you treasure every minute of their babyhood, it flies past all too quickly. The boys were great companions, not inseparable, but fiercely protective of each other's interests. Their inquisitive minds kept my inventive abilities alive. I am firmly of the belief that a child can be alienated from formal learning, possibly permanently, if it is thrust upon him at a too early age. The best learning, during these tender years is that which is subtly put before him and which he trips over in his natural urge to explore and to make sense of his world. So much of this intrinsic curiosity is wasted when formal teaching takes precedence, ignoring the propensity of a child to discover for himself by experiment and imitation.

Nothing teaches the nature of the young human more that one's own offspring for whom one is responsible for twenty-four hours a day. Fine days were always easy to fill, with trips to a park, an adventure playground or in our own garden where large cardboard boxes, planks of wood and things surreptitiously extracted from house or garage became pirates' dens or robbers' hideouts. Wet weather was more of a challenge, but the undoubted star of my ingenuity, according to the boys, was half a pig's head which they espied at the butcher's. They brought it home as a treasured trophy and I have to admit that it repaid its price tenfold as a biological investigation which lasted two inclement days. They were entranced and I ignored the ensuing blood, etc. as much as I could. I had been brought up by a wise mother who, when anyone tended to be inordinately engaged with something which did not really matter, would advise us, "Don't look, dear." This exhortation lasted throughout the most bloody of pig's-head investigations and subsequent, ghoulish descriptions and has, incidentally, proved to be one of the best pieces of advice I would recommend to anyone when stress threatens to overcome one.

My sister was doing supply work, some of it at St Peter's Junior School. There came a time when they were desperate for a teacher to fill in for another staff absence, so it was suggested that I should put my younger son with the excellent lady who looked after his cousin during the day and that my older son should come with us and spend his day in the reception class of the infant department. This met with mixed reactions from my rising four-year-old. He envisaged it as a possibly intriguing adventure – until he saw his class teacher, a nun in the full regalia of her calling.

He had never met with this scene before, but her gentle assurance that there was a lady inside the all-enveloping black seemed to comfort him somewhat, but the object which irrevocably changed his mind was the large red fire engine which he immediately appropriated and, to my shame, refused to relinquish all the time he was there. The only thing he grew to love more than the fire engine was the affectionate tranquillity of his wonderful class teacher.

Shortly after this, my sister was appointed to an inner-city school which had an old building and an adequate playground, but no playing field at all. It was customary, therefore, for classes to be transported by coach to St Peter's, where the playing field was not only huge, but usually dry enough to be played on all the year round as it was on a slight slope. Dawn was supervising games of rounders there one afternoon, when a booming voice echoed across the field from Mr Breen's open window.

"Hey, Dawn, tell your sister if she hasn't got another permanent job lined up yet to come and see me tomorrow."

Which is how my next appointment came about.

I'M A LITTLE WOODEN SPOON

I'm a little wooden spoon, I am, I am, I am.
I don't mind stirring gravy, but can't bear stirring jam;

It colours up my flanges and permeates my wood,
And then I get a scrubbing before I'm looking good.

I know there's one side missing; I traded on that fact,
For once she'd found me lurking, she couldn't put me back.

She thought I looked quite pitiful, it almost made her cry.
But who would tell her what I think? Believe me, it's not I.

I may be old and short and fat, but in the drawer I'm boss.
They may think that I'm uppity. I couldn't give a toss!

I'd been here many years before they joined me in this drawer,
There's long-time spatulas and things, but I was here before.

I go back forty years or so, before her sons were born.
I heard them, whimpering miserably, so pitiful, forlorn.

But then it was I gained the scars of bravery I bear –
From being bashed on playpen rails, on saucepans, on high
    chair.

I wear my decorations still, on top and underneath –
The indentations made back then, by tiny, sharp new teeth.

SPEEDING PIANOS AND
STICKY-BACKED PLASTIC

The two incidents which stand out in my mind of this second period at St Peter's both occurred in the playground. Mr Breen was a jovial head who loved to tease members of his staff gently, never with what could be described as the slightest form of malice, so I suppose it was unfair of us to turn the tables quite so dramatically upon him.

With Christmas approaching, the female members of staff decided to have a quick, celebratory lunch elsewhere, but assured a concerned Mr Breen that we would all be back for the commencement of the afternoon session. We duly departed for a light snack, but could not resist the temptation to provoke our head. As we came back through the gate, we saw him waiting anxiously on the front steps, so promptly linked arms and, swaying precariously towards him, broke into the chorus of 'Nellie Dean', our childish actions greatly amusing the children throughout the playground. Poor Mr Breen. We had to desist and assume an ultra-sober attitude to convince him that he was not facing half a day with half his staff drunk and incapable.

The following summer, both schools on the site, infants and juniors, planned to have a combined celebration in the front playground, as that was the only paved space large enough to accommodate parents, children and staff from the two schools. The junior school was the proud possessor of an iron-framed piano and it was decided that this instrument should be put into its place on the morning of the concert. Moving such a heavy object should be helped by the fact that it was on castors. A team of hefty boys was assembled and they soon manoeuvred the piano across the main hall and crush hall, even down a shallow step. A little increased effort took it up the slope of the playground and across the flat, where the triumph of the furniture removers spurred them on to increase the speed of the instrument hurtling across the tarmac. The architect who had designed the schools and their surrounds had considered that a cobbled area to separate the infant from the junior playgrounds would enhance the project. This may have been the case, but cobbles do not enhance the progress of a racing piano, which promptly embedded its castors between the welcoming stones, while the upper part continued its crazy journey, until it skidded to a halt, shaving a slice off its wooden base. The boys were stricken at what had happened, but somewhat comforted when the base was disinterred and the top replaced. I did not witness the return of the sadly used piano, but heard that some boarding placed across the pebbles had eased its return journey.

While I had been enlarging the population of the world, so the LEA. had been increasing the hours of remedial help for incapable or severely struggling readers. I was now to be allowed eight hours.

A very good friend offered to look after my younger son in term time while I was teaching and the older one was due to start at the local infant school that term. He had already had a taste of schooling, so I anticipated no problems. There were, indeed, none on the first day. He appeared to have enjoyed this new experience of what he termed 'real school', however, he was completely incredulous when told, the next morning, that he had to get ready for school.

"But I've already been to school," he indignantly asserted. It took a lot of convincing a very reluctant child that school would have to be attended not only that day, but for weeks, months and years to come. He was somewhat mollified to learn that Mummy, as a teacher, would also have to go to school for even more years than he did. The idea that I, too, would have to suffer this form of regular incarceration seemed to restore a sense of justice to his world, enabling him to endure formal education with resignation, if not unalloyed willingness.

The boys missed each other, but treasured the weekends with two whole days of indulgence in activities which found favour with parents or, alternatively, of which parents remained blessedly ignorant. For the present, having enjoyed the company of the first son before the second arrived, I now had part of each week with my younger son before he, too, had to attend school.

Those extra three hours I had each week at St Peter's made a difference in that the next echelon of lower reading ages could have a little remedial time, but it was still insufficient to cover the problem adequately. We were now allowed to use the large staffroom, which did improve things considerably. We said goodbye to the interruptions we had suffered from traffic through the crush hall, and when those children not working with me individually or in groups were allowed to sit in comfortable chairs to read quietly, their concentration and enjoyment significantly increased. Another small group, of those children struggling with the vagaries of maths, worked with another teacher at the other end of the room. There was a calm buzz of concentrated work, with a flurry of clearing-away before playtimes, when the staff benefited by having their coffee and tea all ready for them when they arrived.

Again, I was able to act as a supply teacher sometimes, but always had to have advance notice so that I could make alternative arrangements for my sons. When another local school advertised a post which warranted an increased number of hours, I calculated that I would then be able to afford to run a small car, thereby taking on more teaching hours, yet would actually spend more time at home. I had recently passed my driving test and this seemed to be a fortuitous omen; however, the school to which I moved had a very different atmosphere.

The shape of the building was partly to blame for the separate factions which existed and there were, no doubt, historical reasons for the disparity amongst groups of staff. This made my job extremely difficult at times, for I had to extract from each class children according to their need. I adapted my timetable as much as I could to accommodate members of staff, but a friendly solution was almost impossible, as there were underlying objections about which I could only speculate, of which I actually knew nothing and about which I definitely did not want to know. There were no funds available for books or equipment and a large part of my increased income had to be spent on cardboard and other requisites from which I made an ever increasing number of reading games. I did manage to have ordered a roll of transparent plastic with which to cover my endeavours, for the making of them necessitated many hours of work at home.

For some time, I had been aware of some of the distant history of the school, for the one-time headmaster had been a great friend of my grandfather. In the days of that head, individual members of staff were summoned to his study by a prearranged pattern of thumps which echoed throughout the huge pipes of the central heating system. He was, by all accounts, an intimidating figure. That opinion would undoubtedly have been shared by the previous incumbents of the skins and pelts of the stuffed animals and fish which leered at the passer-by in the main corridor. These grizzly remains bore witness to that august gentleman's prowess with lethal gun and line and cast a gloom which seemed to permeate the whole school.

This was the era of the first landing of a man on the moon, so our school, together with others around the city, purchased an enormous television set which had to be installed on its own robust frame and was obviously so heavy that it was quite capable of dealing a final blow to groups of children if it fell on them. There was an exclusion zone duly drawn round its base and, on the historic day, the whole school population assembled in the hall to witness "One small step for a man, one giant leap for mankind."

It was fortuitous that this historic step had been taken before we arrived one morning to find a large, bare stand, devoid of huge television set. One of the outside doors had had its lock broken, but despite the size and weight of the booty, the high, intact fencing round the playing field and the immediate proximity of two busy main roads, that television set vanished forever. This is very puzzling when there are hardly any domestic buildings large enough to accommodate such a thing nationally, let alone locally.

I was not as happy at this present school as I had been at others, but at least there was a small, but convenient room in which to teach my groups and, with my own personal transport I could now ferry more equipment as necessary.

Approaching Christmas, down the trophy corridor came a head whose family I had known for years. On his arm he had threaded three impressive-looking cardboard crowns and I could not resist asking him, "What's this, then, Howard? Promotion?"

I received an equally cheeky remark in exchange, but was surprised when Howard returned a few seconds later and asked for how many hours a week was I paid. When I told him, he said, "Come and join me after Christmas and I'll get you more than that."

I was under the impression that I would have to give the usual notice required, but having been paid on an hourly basis, an hour's notice was all that was required. I was, mercifully excluded from the wrangling that ensued, but the school I was leaving sent me a threatening letter later, telling me that I was to return every bit of the used portion of the roll of plastic covering, as I had illegally taken it from the school. This created something of an impasse, as the letter demanded the return of what was firmly stuck to *my* property. When I pointed this out, the completed games were demanded and I was to be deprived, I thought, of items which had taken me many, many hours to devise and create. This was doubly galling when I remembered how much equipment I had had to buy out of my own money in order to do my job effectively.

Howard told me to leave the matter with him, which I was relieved to do. I heard no more directly, which was not surprising, as Howard had informed my previous head that: "Mrs Dowding is quite willing to return all pieces of covering material, but, at the same time, requests the return of all her lengths of Sellotape attached by her to dilapidated books, and all her pencils, paper, erasers and any other items bought by her and which she left at the school for the benefit of the children."

We heard nothing more.

Robinswood Junior School was a very happy school. Although Howard's custom was to run his school his own way, he backed this up with an almost uncanny ability to pick staff who worked well together, most of them with individual talents which benefited the whole school. There was a purpose-built room which could be made attractive and welcoming and in which I could do the initial testing for reading efficiency. Here there was very little problem with extracting children from classes. I was able to ascertain when class teachers would prefer the presence or, in many cases the absence of particular children and to form my timetable round them.

It was here that I first learnt the advantages of working closely with the educational psychology service who could take an overall view of children whom we saw for only a limited period during the day, yet who could draw on the findings of the many agencies who may have dealt with the whole families. In this school, as in every other, there were problems with children's behaviour which were far more easily understood when the home background was known.

The school was in the centre of a mixed settlement in Gloucester, from large, detached houses to high-rise flats occupied by poorer residents; a truly social mixture.

It was at this time that the local authority required a breakdown of backgrounds, to ascertain which and where were the 'deprived' children. No precise definition of 'deprived' had been formulated, so the research was flawed from the start.

One of the most financially deprived families lived, mother, father and seven children, in a bleak flat in the middle of the estate. The children attended school in barely adequate clothing and were entitled to free school meals – the primary measure by which, officially, deprivation was judged.

The mother attended all the school jumble sales, so we were able to provide her regularly with a huge bundle of clothes of various sizes for which we had charged only enough to avoid her feeling patronised. The brothers and sisters were all mutually supportive, looking for each other at playtimes, approaching the teachers of their younger siblings to ask, "How's our Frank doing, Miss?"

One morning, one of the twins of this family arrived at school covered in what was, obviously a measles rash. I was asked to take him and his ailing twin sister home immediately. I drew up at their block of flats where their mother must have been just inside, for she opened the door as the twins reached it. Without looking beyond them to see how they had arrived home, she opened her arms and hugged the twins, with a devoted expression of love on her face which told such a different story from cold facts of free dinners and jumble-sale clothes.

What arrogance, I thought, to judge deprivation in such a dismissive way, as if tangible wealth mattered more than anything else to a child. Although standard assessment tests were a quick guide to where help was needed, human observation and intuition were what counted in a successful outcome, but a teacher only acquires such expertise with time. I was learning.

FAMILY GROUPING

As the 1960s gave way to the 1970s, Gloucester started to expand. Areas on the outskirts which had previously seen themselves as villages were now taken into the maw of a city. Apart from the western side, bounded by the River Severn, estates crept outwards in all directions, bringing in their wake a need for newly built amenities, including new schools.

The four excellent grammar schools were, and still are, retained within the city, but the blossoming vogue for comprehensive education drove the need for new secondary schools. These were built on the outskirts of the city, but were soon surrounded by the fresh estates from which a good proportion of their pupils would be drawn.

Existing primary schools, whose numbers on roll had been falling, as their locales became occupied by an aging population, now had to expand to fulfil an ever increasing demand for places. So a huge school building plan came to fruition, with some buildings being erected so quickly that their infrastructure showed disastrous flaws before long. The craze for flat roofs had many teachers amassing various containers to catch the inner results of a rainy day before their classrooms became flooded. When one head complained to the building contractors about this regular problem, he felt it quite beyond him to understand their explanation. According to the builders, the leaky roofs had ensued because, being flat and covered in bitumen sheeting, they needed a substantial weight of water on them to seal them sufficiently to prevent leakage. The head was completely unable to elicit a satisfactory answer to his enquiry regarding the cascades of rainwater entering his school through the roof before the required amount of weight was deposited there. There was also the question of whether there would ever be enough water remaining on the roof to activate a seal if most of it was lost via the inside of the building. Flat-roofed schools had workmen swarming over them like bees following an emigrating queen, but an untold number of buckets and bowls remained in service for years.

A short distance from where I was living at the time, a new primary school sprang up, much to the disgust of the local children who had enjoyed that site, splashing in the shallow ponds in summer and sliding on their ice-covered surfaces in the winter. Also on the site had been three horses which, legend had it, made it their life's ambition to bite anyone approaching them. Many of us felt that the danger was the other way around. On our comparatively new estate, swarming with young children, the horses probably suffered the worst trauma, having to share their erstwhile tranquil field with whooping, football-playing humans; great disturbers of the peace. The ponds were drained and a two-storey school sprang up next to the existing playing field. The latter was supposed to provide an amenity for the school, as an extension to the playground, but was soon declared out of bounds when children returned to the classrooms liberally daubed with the results of irresponsible dog-owners.

Dinglewell School was, at first, an all-ages primary provision, with infants in the four ground-floor classrooms and juniors in the first-floor rooms. As usually happens, the school building programme lagged behind the domestic development and all four classrooms were soon full. The head appointed was a convert to the then current idea of family grouping (not to be confused with family planning, as it was often referred to in his speeches designed to convert the under-enthusiastic.) This innovative system involved each of the four classes consisting

101

of children in all infant age groups, leaving the teacher having to cope with children between four and a half and rising eights. It required an intrepid outlook and huge bravery to tackle this method, especially as there were over thirty to each class and one, part-time assistant to share between all four of them.

One teacher, appointed at the opening of the school, had been trained long, long ago and had a most interesting career, including the tuition of children of some of the crowned heads of Europe, making her escape from one belaboured regime in a rowing boat while bullets ricocheted around them. It was obvious, therefore, that she was not easily intimidated, but she coped with this experimental method of teaching in the only way she knew how; she split all the children into their respective age groups and attempted to teach the ensuing four groups simultaneously.

Living so locally, I was aware of the dubious attitude of parents and teachers, but became fascinated to know how it could be made to work. It may have been curiosity, but was more likely creeping financial impecuniosity which made me decide to succumb to the head's repeated pleas to join his infants' staff as an experienced teacher, willing to try anything once.

Both of my sons were now at his school and I felt that I had to stipulate that they would never be drafted into my class. With each of the four classes containing all four age groups, that was no problem and I soon got used to being called "Mummy" up to the school gates and by my formal, school name while on the school premises.

The school had only been opened a term and already problems had arisen. The parents of one fairly severely epileptic boy were extremely keen that he should attend an ordinary school and had been told that it was possible, if they could find a school and a teacher willing to deal with any crisis which may occur. Similarly, an exceptionally bright girl, then six years old, was proving almost untenable in an ordinary school, as she exhibited uncontrollable temper tantrums and resorted to bizarre, sometimes dangerous behaviour when she could not get her own way. I still wonder that I was inveigled into tackling such a challenge.

The school had been built round a small, square enclosure into which the head had introduced ducklings, baby pheasants, quails and chicks, the latter hatched in an incubator while the children watched, in complete wonder. The half-glass doors enabled the infant children in the two centre classrooms to watch these birds growing up, but proved rather a liability in warm weather, as an open door served as an invitation to feathered hordes, much loved, but in danger of being lovingly squashed to death or trodden on in an overcrowded classroom. In common with government predictions and the visions of educational idealists, the rooms had been designed to allow free movement for classes of around twenty, yet had been transformed into crowded spaces of well over thirty, where movement had to be taken with care.

Shortly before I actually took up a teaching post in the infant department, I was accosted by a local lady whom I had known, as a local resident, for quite a few years. She informed me that she had opted for her son (an only child) to start his education in my class, but had one question which caused her concern; "Are you able, as a teacher, to cope with a super-intelligent child?"

For the first, and probably the only time in my life I accessed '*le bon mot*' at the right time. I asked her, "Why? Are you, as a parent, capable of producing one?"

The boy, a handsome, intelligent child, progressed at a phenomenal rate, so perhaps I passed muster in the eyes of his mother.

A huge disadvantage of teaching on one's own doorstep is an inability to enter in the morning or to leave in the afternoon without running the gauntlet of garrulous parents. While a good contact with home can breed the understanding of a child, a constant badgering of a teacher shows little understanding that she also has a life outside school. I therefore undertook to stay late on two evenings a week to meet parents and used my car for the short journey to and from school. This appeared to work quite well and parents were, in the main, content to keep their intrusions for emergencies and for problems which just could not wait.

I had had years of teaching children with special needs and children from deprived backgrounds, but now I found that bright children from relatively affluent homes can have special needs, too. It was shortly after the Christmas holiday and time for planting bulbs which would enhance the classroom with their scent and colours. A large table was covered with a plastic sheet, bowls, water, compost and bulbs at the ready. The children clustered round, smallest in front, all eager to have a turn at soaking and squeezing handfuls of compost to be put into the flower bowls.

One four-year-old boy, habitually dressed in his mother's idea of suitable school garb of white shirt, grey suit and bow tie, shrank away from the table and became quite distressed when the press of larger bodies stopped him escaping backwards. By the time that I had reached him, he was sobbing pitifully and for a few minutes was unable to say what had upset him so.

Eventually, I understood that he had equated bulb compost with 'dirt' and watching people touching it had revolted him. From the earliest time of his understanding he had been conditioned to avoid 'dirt' of all kinds and to preserve himself, his clothes and his surroundings in a perfectly clean environment. I was completely unable to make him understand that compost was not 'dirt', as he understood it, but the necessary medium for plants such as bulbs. Luckily, I forbore to explain this by classing compost as what bulbs liked to eat, a thought which crossed my mind, but fortunately, in the circumstances, remained unspoken.

Later, when I got to know this boy's parents, I could see what attitudes had spawned this aversion to anything not perfect in one's life. Both mother and father had been only children and considered themselves to have been, therefore, greatly privileged. They had each been the focus of their families' attention and, so they proudly informed me, become the sole inheritors of family fortunes. This, they emphatically stated, was to be replicated in the next generation.

Their son would be brought up in a cocoon of cleanliness and an ever-present sense of responsibility to keep himself untainted. The house extension had been modified as a play area where their son could play nicely with every toy imaginable, with no other child gaining access in case, thereby, pollution should enter the area or a piece of expensive equipment get damaged.

I was horrified at the burden foisted onto this child and at the unreal world into which he was being indoctrinated and only thankful that he had, at least, the chance to meet normality at school. Sadly, he remained a solemn and solitary child, always on the periphery of collective activities; an observer, too inhibited to join in. He gained a university place and studied, appropriately, pure maths, and, many years later, has only a tenuous connection with common humanity.

An advantage of the family grouping arrangement was that twins could be taught in parallel classes, so developing their own friends and, arguably individual personalities, while retaining their sibling connections during playtimes. Some parents welcomed this arrangement, but others were determined that their twins should remain as an indivisible unit. The latter attitude, we sometimes felt, was designed to keep alive the reflected glory that the sight of twins, dressed alike, seems to excite in the observers of our society.

No doubt identical twins can elicit a great deal of fun from confusing the rest of us and it was so for the two girls in the next class to mine. In deference to our confusion, their mother put differently coloured ribbons round their dark ponytails, but as those colours varied from day to day and the girls soon found delight in exchanging ribbons, the situation remained as confused as ever. By observing mannerisms, some teachers were eventually able to distinguish between the girls, but we were well behind the other children, very few of whom saw any difficulty at all in distinguishing between them.

One of boy twins was allotted to my class, while his brother was in the next one. They were not identical in looks or personality, but both were attractive and very well liked, by staff and children. They were totally supportive of each other and insisted that they be dressed alike.

As happens in all infant classes, with tummy 'bugs' rampaging at intervals, the twin in my class had an accident which necessitated a change of almost all his clothes, including his shoes. This was no problem, as we always had sets of emergency clothes, in all sizes, to hand. Having a class to cope with, as well as this minor emergency, I wrapped the stained clothes and shoes in newspaper and left the parcel by the boy's coat, ready to be picked up by his mother at home time, which would occur in a few minutes' time. The caretaker, arriving earlier than usual for his evening duties, saw what he thought was a bundle of paper and threw it into the school incinerator. He realised his error when he watched with horror as the paper burned away and the unmistakeable outline of a pair of shoes emerged amidst fragments of fabric. It was the head's unenviable duty to explain to the boy's mother what had happened and to offer for the school to be invoiced for two sets of identical clothes so that the boys could continue their collective attire. The family were very understanding and refused to accept any recompense at all for what they viewed as a genuine mistake, thereby saving school funds many pounds for replacements.

As I had not joined the school until it had been opened for a term, I had had no involvement in what had been ordered in the way of equipment. With my first year's training and subsequent experience, I despaired at what I found. Vast amounts of money had been spent on inappropriate teaching aids, with little regard to the ages and varying abilities of the children and, importantly, the necessity to make sure that all the tiny pieces remained within their relevant unit of equipment – a near-impossible task with a large class in an overcrowded classroom. However, the worst discovery was the reading scheme which had swallowed the majority of the initial budget. I had never seen such an unsuitable piece of publishing erroneously designed to encourage children to read and I know I never will again, for it sank without trace and most teachers never even heard of it. Lucky them.

The only thing in favour of the scheme was that the books were small and could be held in little hands, but the printing, right from the beginning, was too little and the pages were cramped, with illustrations as totally devoid of interest as was the printed material. There seemed to have been very little consideration given to the logical introduction of new words and of similar or contrasting sounds which children need to encounter if they are ever going to be able to build up words for themselves. The whole thing gave the impression of ugliness which failed to arrest the attention. I still wonder at the miracle which enabled some children to learn to read using this appalling material, especially as it gave rise, at times, to children having nightmares. For instance, about halfway through the scheme, there was a vivid account, with accompanying illustrations, of a fire in a stable where horses were trapped. I made a resolution that no more of my class would be subjected to this unthinking publication and only allowed access to the first few books for the time it took me to order, beg, buy or borrow more child-friendly reading books.

One morning, during the following winter, we woke to a white world. Several inches of snow had appeared during the night, covering our part of the country in a fall which made travel extremely difficult, if not impossible. The catchment area was almost totally local then, so the children had little difficulty in crunching, jumping and snowballing their way to school. However, only two of the staff lived within walking distance; one from the junior department and one from the infant – and I was the latter. The only arrangement we could make was for the juniors to be situated in adjoining rooms upstairs and all the infants (about 140 of them) to be together in the school hall until, hopefully, the professionalism of other staff won over their reluctance to undertake such a perilous journey. This procedure worked better than could have been anticipated, with older children taking it upon themselves to help teach and entertain the younger ones. They all revelled in the novelty so much that when individual teachers arrived, exhausted from long walks in deep snow, they were only too pleased to concur with the children's request to stay together in the school hall and share teachers. It worked well for a day, but the later vogue for 'team teaching', where a whole school is, figuratively speaking thrown together, would not have been successful for long in this cramped, unplanned space.

"GO HOME AND WATCH THE BULBS GROW"

It was at this time that I discovered a special, personal talent. So that this shall be a passably accurate account of a career in various aspects of education, I must immediately confess to a sad lack of ability in anything numerical. An ineptitude in arithmetic was the infant and junior forerunner to a complete failure in algebra. I failed to grasp even the bare rudiments of the latter, depending, as it did, on strict orders of procedure, which, struggle as I might, remained a totally unsolved mystery.

To discover, by way of recompense, a special talent for the teaching of reading was a delight. In previous positions, the 'backward readers' as they were then called, had made progress within the groups who came to me, but that had been accounted for, I believed, by the extra attention and individual help which is unobtainable in a full-sized class. Now, however, I had a comparison with other, parallel classes. The four teachers worked closely together and thought nothing of sending an individual or a group of children to another classroom so that all should benefit from the particular expertise of each teacher. Team teaching was an experimental vogue at the time, so the exchange of pupils was not a novel innovation.

Gradually, the children who encountered difficulties with learning to read found their way into my classroom for varying periods of the day, while I gratefully dispensed with those seven-year-olds who had developed a maths ability which needed stretching beyond my natural aptitude.

When I first arrived at the school, I could see no other way in which Family Grouping could be made to work except within an integrated day. So, with great courage, I jumped in with both feet and each day became task orientated rather than time dictated. Each child was given a task book into which, each day, had to be recorded three tasks. These encompassed one involving reading, one based on maths, and one on writing. As each task was presented, it could be marked off and the next day's work assignment entered. Children took their task books home at the weekends, if they wanted to, so the parents could continually follow their offspring's progress.

At first, the chaos that I had imagined inevitably ensued, but gradually, with the older ones helping the younger to adopt the system, it worked extremely well, although it had to be admitted that there was far more carrot then stick. As each child satisfactorily completed the allotted three tasks, it left him or her to spend the rest of the integrated day in a constructional activity of their own choice. Relying on the old truth that teaching is a craft, craftily managed, the constructional activities were educational, but in a fun way. Confidence boosters such as puzzles which could be completed many times with greater proficiency on each occasion were popular with children who preferred to work on their own, while large paintings and construction projects tended to encourage teamwork and an ability to persist in a task which, sometimes, covered weeks of effort.

It was this last need which threw up a huge disadvantage of Family Grouping. While the older children were content to help the younger ones and showed an acquired understanding of immature needs, the restless nature of three or four-year-olds as they go about learning in the active way which is natural to them, spelt disaster for the concentration of the more studiously minded seven-rising-eight-year-olds. When the situation threatened many weeks of constructional activity the atmosphere became potentially murderous. The whole situation was exacerbated by the lack of space for over thirty, mixed-age children in a room designed for twenty who were similarly aged. Something had to be done.

Together with the head, the three teachers discussed the problem and agreed that, while the system worked for the first two years of the child's infant education, something more was needed for those reaching the transition age. They would soon be required to work to a timetable, to complete pieces of work in silence and to conform to the more rigid regime of the junior school.

The older, very experienced teacher had never been happy trying to teach several age groups at once and was delighted with the suggestion that she should take the most mature children under a more formal ambience. The rest of us would continue with the now established practice, thankfully free of the dissension which had ensued from small feet trampling precariously built models, tiny fingers making helpful additions to ongoing artistic projects and naturally exuberant interruptions to studious reading. The innovation made a huge difference to the atmosphere of each room which now became calmer and encouraged cooperation of groups of children of like ability. It also gave the opportunity for the slower seven-year-olds to have a little more time before they faced formality, although this had to be put in ways that could be accepted without loss of dignity or confidence. If a younger sibling was in the same class, this could be used as the reason; they could stay together a bit longer. Some, conscious that were not ready to be under a formal regime, actually asked to stay in the mixed classes. For the rest, we became adept at believable reasoning; we needed, in fact could not do without their help in running the class, their ability in hearing the younger ones read freed the teacher for other tasks, etc. We must have been successful in our subterfuges, as we never had complaints from children or parents.

The abiding memory for those who witnessed the occasion, almost forty years ago, was of watching, in an incubator borrowed by the head, wet, bedraggled chicks hatch and become fluffy yellow balls under the gentle heat. This is the most lasting impression that any of those lucky enough to experience it has retained from their time at that school. It is the first thing they mention when they meet their teacher at the time. How sad that there now seems to be less and less time and attention paid to the wonders of nature but a growing emphasis on the ubiquitous computer.

Although I was happy at that school, I still felt the call of special education. For some, it is like an addictive drug; that satisfaction of achievement one shares with a child who has previously despaired of ever fitting in, of building any degree of self-confidence, of feeling loved or even liked by anybody.

The post of assistant teacher at Longford Special School, whose precursor had been Archdeacon Street where I had taught before I had my sons, was advertised. I applied, was asked for interview and appointed immediately. Flattering, maybe, but it gave me very little time to consider much beyond my natural leanings and, more importantly, the increase in salary that I feared I was soon going to need.

As an attempt at conciliation, we had bought a larger house and I was in the process of redecorating it completely, an occupation I have always greatly enjoyed but which demanded a lot of physical energy – and so did my new job. There were twenty, seven-rising-eights to cope with and a complete absence of any assistant. As there was not yet any provision within the city for children with behaviour difficulties, these tended to be drafted to a school which should have contained only those with intrinsic learning difficulties. The magnitude of the task of coping with such a diverse number and capability of children can only be imagined.

After Christmas, bad weather could be expected, but a classroom whose temperature never rose above fifty-five degrees for days on end was a problem none of us expected. We had glass on three sides of the room, which, allied to persistent frost and frequent falls of snow fostered a totally demoralising atmosphere. The children and I huddled in coats and I begged or borrowed all the reasonably safe forms of heating I could get hold of – after encountering a typically unthoughtful piece of bureaucracy.

The local authority, evidently, had plenty of substitute heating appliances. They were kept in store and could be requested at any time. However, the site of the store was halfway up the Cotswold escarpment and could only be reached via an extremely steep hill – the one which is the first to become impassible in bad weather. So there stayed all the subsidiary heating appliances while children, some of whom had had no breakfast before quite a long journey to school, shivered all day. It has to be the very last resort for a special school to be closed (the staff never join a strike action, either) so we struggled with the adverse conditions, some staff unable to get into school at all and the others risking accidents while driving through snow and frozen slush.

A few months after this wearing experience and a domestic situation which was fast deteriorating, I had to own that I was trying to cope with more than I could endure. I could not eat or sleep: even thinking logically was getting beyond me and I had to acknowledge that I needed help.

This resulted in a strict lecture from the wise doctor who had known me all my life and an even stricter instruction to stop shouldering so much responsibility and to "Go home and watch the bulbs grow."

So I did.

PAUSE FOR REFLECTION

For the next few weeks I enjoyed seeing my sons off to school and performing, at a leisurely pace, all those domestic chores which for years had been done at breakneck speed.

There was even time for one of my abiding loves, tending a garden. It was here that I felt the power of natural healing restore me, as the stress under which I had long been labouring gradually slipped away. I saw the bulbs flower and fade and perennials take their place. There was time to relax on a newly mown lawn and to savour the scent of roses mixed with the acid aroma of cut grass.

There was so little demanded of me, that to do the shopping, wash and clean and then meet the boys from school became part of a renewal, a recuperation. And yet – as the washing blew on the line, at playtime the voices of the children at the local school floated on the wind and brought back the memory of so much shared enjoyment.

I was beginning to feel deprived, to miss being a part of something which is important in every child's life; discovery of the world which is driven by a natural curiosity. An urge to take part in helping this process slowly regrew within me, as I remembered incidents, funny and touching – sometimes both. Pictures, sounds, incidents began to haunt me. A voice, calling me back to school at first whispered softly, but became more insistent as memories flooded back.

The strange, integrated day had been a challenge and,

until the older children were separated into a more formal atmosphere, somewhat chaotic. There could be no set pattern to the day, no response to the sounding of bells except the necessary ones for breaks, lunchtime and the end of the school day. A visitor to the classroom may have taken the view that the whole thing was unwieldly, yet, with a great deal of faith and organisation which was subtly planned, that visitor would have been disappointed if he or she wanted to find a child who was not gainfully employed. Each one was always busy, with those who were less competent able to elicit help from those who were coping better. The main advantage, which none of us had fully foreseen, was the freedom for a child to master a particular skill in an astoundingly short time. Although each had to complete the set of three tasks, a particular child could return to a favourite type of learning as a 'constructional activity' if they so chose.

The memory of Martin remains with me still. He came to the class just before his fifth birthday and was drawn to books as an iron filing to a powerful magnet. He was bright and quick, so his maths and writing tasks were accomplished in record time. Apart from PE sessions and broadly organised games, Martin read. At first he selected picture books from the library corner and related what the illustrations told him, but he soon grew dissatisfied with this and started asking, "What do the words say?"

If I was not immediately available, he would demand an answer from the nearest, competent classmate, pointing with a tiny finger at the words and repeating them to himself. For almost six weeks, Martin became my constant shadow, often clutching the back of my dress, partly to prevent him crashing into things as he held his current book in front of him and partly to have a ready answer when he encountered new words. He did not mind the amusement caused by his constant shadowing, for books had become his passion and the act of reading his only interest. He took his book into the playground and, while all the other children milled around him, he sat on a seat or a patch of grass, contentedly reading. Now and again he would grab a passer-by to ask him what a particular word said, then retreat again into his own little world.

Martin joined in the word-building techniques I taught to those who were ready to use them, but I could tell that he was humouring me and had found his own way round the vagaries of printed English. He had devised his own methods of comparison and had sorted out similarities and differences in words. Almost alone he had reached the stage where many new words could be guessed at with some accuracy by their context. We were already impressed, but when, at the end of so few weeks I tested his reading age, I found it to be in excess of seven and a half. Not bad for a child of just over five.

I have wondered, ever since, how many children, with constant and immediate help on tap as they needed it would achieve the skill of reading so painlessly and quickly. It is possible that we hamper progress by trying to teach reading by the way which seems logical to us, as adults.

When Martin, having learned to read to his satisfaction, transferred his gargantuan attention to maths, I transferred him to the class of a much better mathematician than I, where he attacked his new subject with the same single-mindedeness. Some children are just destined for the best and most demanding universities.

The first day at school is often traumatic. I can remember my own when, after the lunch break, I joined the wrong line of children making their way back to the classroom. I had hardly entered the room when the teacher leapt at me, literally lifting me into the air and, admonishing me, "You don't belong in here, little girl," deposited me back into the hall and shut the classroom door on me. Because I could not remember beyond which high, brown door I had been welcomed that morning, I was terrified and ran, crying, back out of the lofty entrance where, luckily, my aunt was still chatting to a friend.

As that memory made me realise how any child may feel on their first day, I always made a point of being extra-attentive and reassuring to each newcomer. Usually, in a local school, there are one or two familiar faces and a new child can be distracted by an interesting piece of apparatus or an intriguing activity. There are very few tears from the children, although one's emotions are disturbed by the number of mothers blindly sobbing their way back across the playground.

However, this sympathy soon disappears when those same mothers appear at playtime, with their tear-stained faces pressed between the railings, needing to reassure themselves that their little darlings are missing them. They seem not at all comforted by the sight of their progeny happily playing with new friends while grudgingly affording a perfunctory wave towards them.

One small boy, already notorious for belonging to a renownedly aloof family, was deposited at my classroom door, clothing uncreased, hair plastered down and clutching an enormous satchel. Wondering if the family would be satisfied with the small amount of equipment required to be toted by a five-year-old, I said, as I had to all the others, "Mummy will be back at dinner time. Sit down and we will find you something nice to do." To my surprise, he did nothing of the sort, but tipped his head back, looked me in the eye and told me to "P*** off!"

The classroom went completely silent as I, believing that every dog is, as the saying goes, entitled to one bite, asked him, "I beg your pardon. What did you say?"

He replied, "Alright, then, f*** off!"

There was the sound of the intake of breath throughout the room, then complete silence while all the other children waited to see what I would do.

It has always been my belief that anyone can choose to behave, or to speak, however they choose, provided that they are prepared to undergo the consequences, so the now grinning young man was lifted bodily from the room, put outside the door with his chair and table and told that, while he was at liberty to say what he liked, I was not prepared for the other children and staff to have to listen. Regaining my breath and, I hoped, a little dignity, I expressed sorrow that he had to stay outside and that we would all be happy to have him with us again when he was saying things we wanted to hear.

There began one of the worst mornings I have ever experienced. He repeatedly came into the room, uttering expletives, but his swaggering gait had definitely flagged a bit by lunchtime.

When he went home for lunch, I realised how my arms ached from dealing with a struggling, swearing, kicking child, but I felt much worse when he did not return to school in the afternoon. I imagined the headlines in the press: "Teacher Victimises Small Child" – or much worse. I had told the headmaster exactly what had happened, although this was largely unnecessary as the volume of a small boy in full swearing flood had been information enough.

The small boy did not appear for afternoon school and I envisaged his parents in earnest consultation with a local education officer or, worse still, a solemn solicitor.

As afternoon school came to a close, I saw with horror that the small boy was waiting for me outside my classroom with his mother and very large father. There was, thankfully, no sign of anyone who looked like a solicitor.

After all the other children had departed, I could put off the encounter no longer, but before I could say anything, father boomed, "We have come to apologise to you, Mrs Dowding, for sending such a rude boy to your class. The only thing I would plead in his defence is that he did have the courage, eventually, to tell us what he had said to you."

The little lad had, obviously, had an unforgettable afternoon and was now standing there, tear-stained and chastened.

His father continued: "I have warned him, that if he continues to behave like this, he would find himself in court one day with someone like me *trying* to defend his behaviour."

So – the law had come down on my side and those parents became the most supportive pair I have ever encountered; and their son? The last I heard of him, he had just become a QC.

While I was at that school, a newly qualified teacher was

appointed. He was a friendly, competent young man to whom the children took immediately. His popularity was even more enhanced when he brought into school the mynah bird which had lived in digs with him and three other students. The bird needed no introduction, as he shrieked, at frequent intervals, "I'm Napoleon", thus keeping his presence felt throughout the school. Each class, of course, longed to house Napoleon, while he delighted in the sight of new faces round his cage each day. When he became unduly excited, his language became as ripe as one would expect after living with raucous students for three years, so a black cloth was ever ready to be flung over the cage, as the method by which Napoleon could be rendered silent. The staff proclaimed that Napoleon needed a rest, but the children were not fooled and enjoyed the occasional outburst heard before the application of the black cloth.

Napoleon particularly looked forward to a teacher calling the names on the register and interjected his own name with such volume that it almost drowned out the laughter of the children.

His visit gave rise to other pets being brought in and we often had a good selection of small animals in our rooms. Uncaged ones had to be banned, as there was a danger of them being stepped upon, but hamsters, gerbils and guinea pigs encouraged an interest in wildlife beyond the birds in the aviary at the centre of the school. Pets were observed, fed, watered and cosseted, then the strictest teacher decided to base an art lesson on the drawing of small animals. This was a mistake, as pets were placed as models in the centre of tables and pools spread from the centre of tables, much to the delight of the small artists. Sadly, the portraiture had to come to an abrupt end, but remained a cherished memory for many of us.

These were the pictures which kept returning to me ever more vividly and I knew that I must get back to where I belonged – in a classroom.

LIFTING AND SINKING

By sheer luck and good timing, the post of "Teacher of backward readers" at the school where I had been happiest became vacant. Tucked under the foot of Robinswood Hill, it took its name from that landmark. Infant and junior departments were built as adjoining units with the kitchen and dining areas in the middle. The long buildings, single storied for infants and double for juniors, looked out upon a huge playing field on the other side of which was an ancient oak. The latter had been a feature of Matson long before the school existed and was dearly loved by the children. For all of us, it seemed to personify continuity; it had remained there as had several generations who lived in flats and houses and mixed with families who had been resettled when whole communities had been moved from Lower Westgate Street and other over-crowded areas.

My grandmother, who had taught swimming for many years at Gloucester Baths, knew the surnames and backgrounds of the majority of these families and could regale me with tales of generations stretching back a century or more. Some were descended from barge families who had, at last, been persuaded to desert their wandering life style, while others had moved into the city to seek the employment which shrank as farms became increasingly mechanised.

It was an area of old-fashioned loyalties, of looking after one's own and closing ranks when necessary.

A couple of stories circulated through the estate, told with admiration for the audacity of particular residents and varying attitudes towards the law.

Another school in the area had been burgled and a small amount of cash taken. A window had been broken and a trail of drops of blood led across the staffroom, into the secretary's office, where the haul must have been disappointingly tiny, then out again through a side door, through the estate and up the stone steps of one of the block of flats. When the local police followed the trail, they were not surprised to have the door opened by a man who sported a large, bloodstained tea towel round his arm. The thief, however, still obviously under the influence of last night's indulgences, expressed wonder at the law's ability to trace him and was accompanied to the local police station still mumbling his admiration.

There was a small row of shops near one end of the estate, while at the other a branch of the Co-op did a steady business – stacking its daily takings in a safe until they could be taken to the bank. This represented a bonanza to several of the local residents, many of whom were unemployed. Breaking into the Co-op one night presented no problem, but safe cracking was not within their repertoire. After a considerable time trying to open Pandora's box, they had to admit defeat. Having reached the safe, however, it seemed a pity just to turn their backs on it and go home, so they decided to take it with them in the hope that it could be opened when they had more time, light and, hopefully, expertise. Between them they could just about lift the safe, but no way could they carry it through the estate to where it could be hidden. However, road workers had left tools and equipment further up the road, so it took only minutes to fetch a stout builder's wheelbarrow and a few more to heave the safe into it.

Builders' barrows are not noted for their silent progress, but the troop managed the journey all the way past the mostly sleeping population and the local police station up to a block of flats. It can only be conjectured how they managed to manoeuvre the heavy safe up two flights of stairs and into what they considered a 'safe' house.

In the morning, the absence of the safe, the telltale marks of the barrow's wheel and the barrow's continued presence by a block of flats told the story quite plainly. The edges scraped off the stone steps for the first two flights of stairs continued the trail up to a particular door. The only apparent occupant of the flat, a woman still in her nightclothes, was a little reluctant to let in two policemen, who soon spotted a large, rectangular shape, draped with a sheet, in one corner of the living room. Their enquiry as to what the shape might be, elicited the answer, "Oh, I asked my man to bring me something to put our budgie's cage on and he brought me that. I've got no idea what it is, but it does the job, don't it?"

As is a trait in Gloucestershire, many parts of the city still hold this ability to stand together and it was largely due to this that Robinswood School owed a lot of its success. Its other great assets were its headteachers. The head of the infant department had been a colleague of mine at the special school and had a deep understanding of young children, showing a firm hand behind a loving attitude which was always fair and constant. It had come as no surprise that she had been asked to house, within her school, a special unit for 'maladjusted' children, who had, until then, either been uncomfortably contained in normal schools or, if that became impossible, drafted to special schools which were not really suitable to cater for their individual needs. After a few teething problems, the unit settled into the school and enriched the lives and the understanding of all the children.

The head of the junior department had been appointed when the school was first opened and, although perhaps I should not put it on record as I was one of them, he had a fantastic knack of appointing members of staff who effortlessly worked together in harmony. He always gave full backing to his staff in front of anyone else. He may have needed to take individuals to task later, in private, but to the outside world we were totally united under a head who treated us all, teachers, assistants, parents, children and visitors with unfailing courtesy. This attitude flowed throughout the school; when it was noticed that the head stepped aside to allow a female member of staff, or a girl pupil, to enter a room first, it became quite normal for the boys to follow suit, so that with no pressure, but with an excellent example, good manners became something to be copied and desired. At the end of the day, the head was invariably by the main door, with a word for each child as they left. When a child wished him "Goodnight, Dad," in an absent-minded way, it almost brought tears to his (and our) eyes. It encouraged us to think that here was another little charge who had found something with us that he or she found sadly lacking in their home lives. Many came from homes where there was only one parent, or perhaps where 'uncles' came and went, each with their own idea of how children should behave and how they should be treated or, sadly, excessively punished. That they found a sense of security and continuity at school was, indeed an achievement.

By the time that I returned there, a small room had been equipped with bookshelves and quite a few books had accumulated as the room was also now used as a little library. For more comprehensive facilities, we took groups of children to the excellent nearby public library.

It was decided that I would concentrate on the pupils whose reading quotient was the lowest, so I tested the reading age of all those who gave concern to their class teachers and compared reading age with chronological age. The main principle could not be strictly adhered to, as any experienced teacher will tell you, there are some children who are able to progress only at a very slow pace in any academic studies and most seem quite happy to do so. It borders on cruelty continually to compare them with the general average. If they are progressing at their own, maximum pace, they should not be saddled with education's obsession with testing and comparisons. I put such children onto my timetable to come to me once a week so that they would not feel left out and so that I could make sure they would benefit from any potential upturn of speed. Apart from that, it was logical to concentrate on the youngest ones. There is a group of children who seem to attain a sudden maturity when they are transferred from infants to juniors and can show surprising progress in their first year under a more formal regime. Some gain confidence because of the widening of the curriculum, with drama, sports and art acting as spurs, so this first year is often a time of great progress.

With such a cooperative staff, it was easy to arrange a time when I could extract children to concentrate on their reading ability without disrupting the running of the class, but there were exceptions.

One boy came to us aged eight. He spoke no English. He had newly arrived in this country and knew only Polish. As usual at that age, he soon picked up some of our native language, as usual, starting with the more undesirable words learnt in the playground, but it was hard for him to fit in. For some reason, he became fascinated with the way that some children left the classroom and disappeared for a time. One day, determined to solve this mystery, he marched out with the leaving group and presented himself in my little reading room.

He must have sensed my intended rejection, for he said, in a determined way, "I stay," backing up his statement with drawing up a chair beside me and sitting upon it. Determination was written all over his face and a thirst for knowledge is irresistible, so there he stayed for the lesson.

I was aware that he was soaking up everything the other children were doing, craning to see the words they were reading and obviously benefiting from being with us.

At the end of the session, the group were ready to give way to the next, but my Polish friend sat stolidly in position and repeated, "I stay," so I sent a note to his teacher to explain the situation.

The understandable answer came back that I could keep him indefinitely, as it was the first sign of him actually being able to learn anything and an activity which increased his knowledge of English could not fail to be a good thing.

So – there he sat, refusing a personal reading book, but listening avidly to everything which went on around him. Out of the corner of my eye, I sometimes caught his lips moving as he silently tried out the pronunciation of words as a child read them out loud. He refused to take part in any of the reading games, dearly loved by the other children; just watched with undivided attention. He was a solemn lad, but his concentration showed how much it meant to him to be there with us.

Then one day, he brought a book with him, sat beside me as usual, but instead of listening to what the other children were reading, he banged his book on the table and said, in a determined voice, "I read this."

My heart sank. It was the account of the sinking of the Titanic; not a version written for children, but very long, with small print and quite technical language. I tried my best to deflect him from such a task, for by now he had some understanding of English, but he would not be deterred. So there he sat, a constant presence for weeks, patting my arm when he wanted to know a word, which was painfully frequent at first, but, like the child who, at four, had found his own way to learn to read, so my Polish friend persevered. He never got bored and, several weeks later, when, to my great relief, he had turned the last page of *The Sinking of the Titanic*, he accepted my suggestions for his further reading. This one-on-one method is certainly draining, but it reaps remarkable results and no doubt accounts for the assertions of children learning to read before they went to school. If a parent were always available and a child that way naturally inclined, what an advantage it conferred upon a four year-old. Unfortunately, some theorists believe that every child is ready to read at a certain prescribed age, and by a certain prescribed method, but many incidents of acute anxiety have proved this not to be the case.

LITERARY HASSLE

I could be having a lie-in,
   I could be lounging in bed,
But I have to get down on computer
   What's gyrating around in my head.

There's washing to do, and the ironing,
   (The basket has long overflowed).
But there's no time to deal with the mundane.
   The muse prods at me like a goad.

The family's gathering Sunday.
   There's a socking great gammon to bake,
A blancmange and a jelly and trifle
   And their favourite chocolate cake.

There's my book – halfway written and stagnant.
   The notes and research are all done.
Dissertations on being dyslexic
   And trying to make it more fun.

I should be out tidying the garden
   And zapping recalcitrant weeds
Which, thriving on long inattention,
   Are busy distributing seeds.

I could plead incompetence, headaches,
   I could be pig-headed, perverse,
But I'll rise to the challenge – so help me.
   And get down to writing some verse.

BACK TO ROBINSWOOD

Occasionally, when a teacher was absent unexpectedly, there was an interim period until a supply teacher could be obtained to fill the vacancy. I was frequently asked to fill that gap, but pleased that it was only for very short periods, as it meant leaving my primary task of helping the struggling readers. However, with the increased number of hours allotted to my job, I could now afford to run a car, which made a big difference to the length of my working day, so that some supply work, as long as it did not impinge upon my regular job, was very welcome. I knew the school and the children – they knew me, so this arrangement was much easier than going 'cold' into a totally strange environment. From experience in playground and dinner duties, I found that I could predict which children would be potential troublemakers in class (given the chance) and so was able to make sure that they were too occupied to have time for perpetrating tricks, which often happened when a relief teacher was totally unfamiliar with the children.

Usually, when an innocent supply teacher enters the classroom and asks the class about the lessons for the day, the question elicits, "Miss, we haves PE" or "It's art and craft all day, Miss" or, more daringly, "We spends the day outside playing football/skipping/playing."

It is always safest to obtain a timetable before entering a strange classroom, for maths and English will not appear by request.

During the arranged and fairly long absence of one member

of staff, the local education authority sent a supply teacher to cover the vacancy. We had rarely met such a totally nice, dedicated man. He was full of innovative ideas and enthusiasm and we felt, initially, that the children would be sorry to see their own teacher back.

As is usual, the first day went well, with the children biddable under his new, fascinating regime. They were consulted, listened and acceded to. Subjects were introduced in intriguing ways which were supposed to keep them 'on task'; indeed, for a few days these methods seemed to be working, for the children were reciprocating with their own plans. Either they continued with what they wanted to do with their time, or the more crafty were devising ways in which their enthusiastic teacher could be hoodwinked.

Inevitably, with this licence came boredom and then mayhem, for lack of any discipline leaves a vacuum which children are always capable of filling in their own, inimitable way.

The noise emanating from the classroom spread along the corridor and even down the stairs. Short visits from other teachers calmed the situation temporarily, but the over-kind, shapeless regime rendered the situation impossible. At last, this kindly, inventive teacher admitted defeat and left the school. We all wished him well and hoped that he would find a more sympathetic, receptive group of children, but could not envisage where this might be.

This left a class grown out of control and no teacher until another, more competent supply could be found. The head requested one immediately, but in the meantime asked me if I would fill in the times when he was unable to be with them. Always willing to take a challenge, on the understanding that failure would not count permanently against me, I volunteered to enter the lions' den.

I love children dearly, but I do not always like them. This fact the children soon found out when they were given to understand that the class, henceforth, would dance to my tune – not theirs. I am sure that it was not purely imagination that there settled upon the children a sense of relief. At last they again knew where they were, what was acceptable, where the limits were, so that complete confidence was assured within those limits.

Using a carrot, as well as a metaphorical stick, I promised an interesting afternoon if all required, formal work had been completed by the end of the morning. Not only was this aim reached, but it was accomplished in a blessed near-silence, except for slower children being helped by those who were more able so that the afternoon's activities would take place.

I had planned chalk and pencil rubbings outside, but heavy rain put paid to that idea, so, having prepared the paper and other requirements, it had to be an indoor activity. First, we closed our eyes and relied on our fingers to explore surfaces. After a few undercover, illicit explorations of a personal nature had been severely discouraged, the children got quite enthralled with this other way of 'seeing' the world and with the methods by which we could turn it into visual patterns. When it permitted crawling under desks to record the floor surface, even the boys were intrigued. Then the interest spread to the walls and the concrete landing surface and there was quite a competition to see who could get the clearest, most interesting pattern, with the children autographing their efforts and pinning them up on the wall.

We were to have a competition to see how many each of us could identify before we went home.

It was almost time for this final activity, while I was on my stomach, under a table, pencil-rubbing a rather interesting woodgrain, when the head came up to relieve me, sure that I would have had enough. I heard his voice and emerged from under the table to see a look of absolute relief spread across his face. He told me afterwards that, upon seeing so many of the class lying quietly prone, then being unable to see me, he dreaded what may have happened. All sorts of things, usually found in science-fiction literature, had flooded through his mind. He had managed to obtain a supply teacher who would start in the morning. She was a capable lady who had filled in for absences before, so the class would be continuing on a calm, even keel again.

Shortly after this, it was decided to take the whole school to the Malvern Agricultural Show. This was an excellent project, as so many city children grow up with no first-hand knowledge of farm animals and of where their food comes from. We were to have four coaches, with two teachers on each and the head acting as a 'floater' which, as it transpired, was a great mistake. I sat at the back of our coach so that I could enunciate a disembodied command to "Sit down" wafting down the coach if a head should have the temerity to rise above the seat. There were no seat belts then and the very small children were placed three to a two-part seat, so strictly remaining in seats was necessary for their safety and our sanity.

It was a glorious day, not too hot, but without a cold wind. The picnic lunch, prepared in the school kitchen, was universally voted excellent and, due to the veto on the carrying of more than a very small amount of pocket money, there was no grizzling. In fact, everyone had a lovely and instructive day. Helpfully, there were flags hoisted high at one side of the show ground and we had made sure that each child knew which flag to make for when it was time to come back to school. A few of the smallest children were so overwhelmed by the size of the ground, the strangeness of the exhibits and the thought of perhaps becoming lost, that they became a little frightened. They soon recovered, however, with the registration number of their own coach written on the back of one hand and the telephone number of the school on the other. Thus equipped, they felt able to enjoy the day.

When it was time to return to the coaches, every single child was there on time, tired, but thrilled with the day's experiences. We climbed into our transport, counting the children again, just to make sure that no-one was inadvertently left in Malvern, then, with the two teachers to each coach, they drew off the car park, with our coach exiting last.

Luckily, some of the children looked back to get their final glimpse of the exhibits they had found so fascinating. A concerted cry of "Miss, Miss, there's Mr Watts running after us," arose as we looked, through the rear window at the increasingly distant figure of the headmaster. Despite his astonishing speed, there was no possibility that he would have caught up our coach if he had not been spotted. The way he was greeted after the coach driver had stopped and waited for him, was proof of the affection he inspired in the children.

The outing gained a new title. The teachers had been planning to do all sorts of activities around 'The Malvern Agricultural Show', but we were fighting a losing battle, for the day was known at the school for evermore as 'The day we lost our headmaster'.

Shortly after this, Mr Watts attended the local education office – a rare occurrence which caused much speculation amongst the staff. He did not return until after school had finished for the afternoon, but as soon as I arrived the next morning, I was asked to go to his office. My main conjecture was that another 'rationalisation' had been put into practice and that I, as the only part-timer, would be the victim. So it was with a heavy foreboding that I entered the room. When I saw the expression on Howard's face, I thought that I had guessed right. He looked embarrassed and, uniquely, seemed lost for words.

He asked me to sit down and confessed that he had done something dreadful and that he hoped that it would work out all right in the end. I began to envisage not only embarrassing possibilities, but illegal, even fatal actions. It then transpired that I was the one who could solve what was, according to him, a dreadful situation in which he had put himself. What did he want me to do? I had known him and his family for many years, but I could not imagine why I had been singled out to save him from whatever it was that he dreaded so. As he still remained tongue-tied, I tried to fight the involuntary pictures which sprang to my mind, like burying a body, or, at least, standing in court and having to lie to save him from whatever fate he was obviously facing.

At last, Howard found the words to explain the situation.

He had been summoned to the local education office where

he had received a request (a nice way of framing a directive) to house a special unit within his school. The infant unit had been very successful, but some children within it had already stayed in that department an extra year and needed to move on. There was also a growing need for appropriate provision for older children and it seemed logical to have a junior unit within the same school complex. This appeared to me to be a sensible move and, as our numbers were likely to fall slightly after the next September, a classroom could be made available for the venture. As Howard went on explaining how he had agreed with the project, he covered accommodation, numbers, transport, teacher conditions, etc. then asked me what I thought. I had no hesitation in agreeing that the idea looked quite viable and that I would look forward to seeing it work.

When Howard's face lit up and relief spread across his features, I was half prepared for his exclamation: "Thank God for that. I told them I would agree to it as long as you would take the unit."

No wonder he had been dubious about what he had been up to. We never got him to own up to what he would have done if I had immediately turned down the offer. As it was, I asked for a few days to think about it, as, of course it would be full-time and experience had already taught me that special education requires far more than time and know-how. It is emotionally draining, makes huge demands on one's home life in the way of preparation, meetings and home visits but no other branch of teaching can hold the potential for such a sense of achievement.

My sons were now at the local school and my mother or aunt was always willing to be with them when they were not well or when our holidays did not coincide. The prospect of a new challenge, as the first 'Teacher in Charge of the Special Junior Unit for Maladjusted Children', as the official job title proclaimed, literally made my mouth water.

SIR LANCELOT, OH, LANCELOT

Sir Lancelot, brave Lancelot, of Lady Guinevere,
Who, Arthur occupied with war, sneaked in for 'that there 'ere'.

Sir Lancelot, oh, Lancelot, why do I swoon and pine?
How can I break down your defence, persuade you to be mine?

Oh, Lancelot, dear Lancelot, what are your ageless charms
Enticing me to be ensnared in metal-cladded arms?

Oh, Lancelot, Sir Lancelot, your casing quells my heat
Especially when I think of spurs entangled in the sheet.

Dear Lancelot, Sir Lancelot, with heaving chest unseen
How can we consummate our love with armour in between?

Sir Lancelot, my Lancelot, I have bolt cutters ready
And should you step within my bower, I'll try to keep them
    steady.

Oh, Lancelot, you must contain your ardour overnight,
For iron is tough and hard and sharp – and chain mail's knitted
    tight.

Ooooh, Lancelot, Sir Lancelot, restrain your natural urge
Until, all reinforcements gone, our bodies can converge.

Sir Lancelot, bare Lancelot, as dawn comes redly creeping,
This metalwork has tired me out – I'll spend the next hours
    sleeping.

HERE WE GO

In setting up the special unit in the junior school we enlisted the help of the head of the infant department who had run an extremely effective unit for several years. She was particularly pleased that we were to continue the work she was doing so successfully, especially as a few of her unit children had reached the grand old age of eight and were, therefore, technically juniors. One of these was also unusually big for his age and was consequently acquiring added behavioural difficulties. It was galling for him and for others of junior age to be amongst infants, some as young as four plus and this was fast giving rise to the negation of any benefit they derived from being in a special unit.

A very important aspect of the junior unit was that it would be an integral part of the school, not to be viewed as an 'add-on'. It would be sited in the centre of the building, in an ordinary classroom and the children would integrate fully at all possible times. Although at first this seemed to take some of the responsibility away from the teacher in charge, in reality this increased her work, especially at first. At the end-of-term staff meeting, Howard made it clear that any disputes, unacceptable behaviour or doubts about how a situation should be handled must be referred to me. I felt a terrific burden being placed upon my shoulders, but I should have had more faith in the extensive experience of a headmaster who had considered all possible situations.

It was soon obvious that his wisdom had eased my task of

making the unit a success, as I became the sole judge of the best way to handle the children within my care, wherever a problem arose. The teaching staff immediately accepted it, but some of the auxiliary staff, not understanding the backgrounds of some of the more difficult children, attempted to solve playground altercations as they would with the rest of the school population which, in many cases, made things much worse and could have had a damaging effect if allowed to continue.

All the children referred to the special unit had had difficulties settling into ordinary classroom situations, not to mention the difficulties some schools had experienced in trying to assimilate them into their working routines.

The records coming up with the infant children were precise and written in the phraseology easily understood by those in special education. I read them with the greatest of interest, realising that I must find out in the case of each child, what had worked and, more importantly, what had not. The purpose of the unit was to help each who had never 'fitted in' to become, wherever possible, a child able to cope in an ordinary classroom for the rest of his or her formal education.

I was firmly convinced that to achieve any degree of success, mistakes of the past must not be repeated. This was truly where I must live up to the educational saying that teaching is ninety-nine per cent acting and one per cent know-how. I fervently hoped that, with experience, the acting would become less demanding as the know-how faction subsequently improved.

Records from other schools were not so easy to decipher in their content, as they were written by often hard-pressed teachers who had had their classes severely disrupted by one of my soon-to-be recruits. In some of these files, there was a sense of desperation, of a teacher having tried everything she could think of to integrate a particular child into its classroom surroundings, while at the same time having to teach around thirty other children, most of whom wanted to cooperate and to learn. If, in their desperation, they had tended to dwell solely on the negative aspects, I could not blame them. Any teacher who genuinely cares about the progress of all her charges will naturally grow to resent the inordinate amount of time which has to be devoted to a child with perpetually challenging behaviour. It is natural, for her duty is to her class and it amounts to a dereliction of that duty if thirty children receive a decidedly patchy education while a disproportionate amount of her time and energy are taken up attending to just one who experiences severe learning and/or behavioural difficulties. So I read between the lines at times, trying to see beyond the frustration and to form a picture of that child as a person.

This proved to be somewhat of a mistake, as many entries to my unit appeared to bear no resemblance to the picture I had formed from reading cold records. As time went on, experience told me to read carefully the top page, which listed medical history and requirements with the greatest of care then to wait until I knew a child before I waded through the opinions of others.

This was not born of arrogance, but of the resolution to treat each child as a little person with a unique personality, yet who needed to conform enough to fit into society. I was convinced that acceptable behaviour would follow. I would have to help each child to assess the possible outcome of his or her actions which could help them to develop restraint in order to reach the eventual desire.

As I read these personal records, it was borne in upon me what a responsibility I had taken on. It was not immediately obvious how a little outcast, rejected repeatedly and with antisocial behaviour could be led into a self-confident life of personal achievement, but I resolved to try my best.

The unit was designed to hold no more than eight children at a time although later we had as many as eleven or as few as three and experienced no correlation between the number of children in the unit and staff exhaustion. Just one in the full throes of a destructive temper tantrum could be more tiring than a score of conformers.

I was entitled to a full-time assistant – an essential element in such a unit, as many times a teacher is forced to give her undivided attention to one child and needs an assistant to carry on with the normal routine. An assistant was an invaluable adjunct in another crucial field. It was only a partial success if a child learnt to behave acceptably within the sheltered precincts of the school, but agreeable behaviour had to continue as second nature outside as well. The presence of an assistant meant that we could make frequent forays into the bigger world, being provided with sufficient supervision and, more importantly, two pairs of vigilant eyes.

When I had first returned to teaching after the birth of my sons, the younger one was not yet at school. A friend whom I had known for some years and whose common sense and firm yet fair attitude I admired had looked after him for a few hours a week. I felt that her attitude, energy and natural talents were just what the unit needed. Apart from that, with so much else being new to me, to have an assistant who was a friend and therefore somewhat predictable, would make the initial running of the unit much smoother. I would not be able to share detailed confidential records and events with Anne, but her common sense radiated normality.

During what those who are not involved in education term 'the long summer holiday' I spent many hours searching through catalogues and trying to get the best value for the sparse two hundred pounds which had been allotted as the start-up funding for the unit. The cost of paint to redecorate a dismal classroom had to be a personal concern as was the actual labour, but by the time that September came, we had a bright, colourful room, complete with bookcases, tables and chairs from around the rest of the school, a carpeted area courtesy of a friendly retailer, various plants from cuttings raised for the room and a smattering of educational material specifically designed for the unit's purpose. The ambience was welcoming and, having spent so much time already there, I felt at home despite the task we had ahead of us. Nevertheless, echoes of extracts from some of the records of my future charges haunted me.

One boy, coming to me at the age of seven, had been excluded by four schools and numerous fostering homes. This rejection, where his sister had been accepted each time had rendered James into a truculent, uncooperative child who trusted no-one and yet cried silently for attention. He had even resorted to repeatedly soiling his bed, clothes, the walls of his room and the foster home's bathroom with faeces after discovering what attention this directed towards him.

Revolting behaviour and personal attention had become a way of life for him, as he knew no other. He had no memory of being appreciated for who he was, only for the bad things he did. As I read his records, in a file already several inches thick, I could see that James was to present a huge problem.

Another boy, who had a twin sister, had come into the infant department with almost no power of speech. The two children had been kept almost exclusively from birth, in a bedroom, receiving the very minimum of care and parental contact. They had developed a basic language of their own, but devoid of any outside stimuli had very little awareness of normal human behaviour. The girl was surprisingly adaptable and, within two years of nursery and infant attendance, fitted in with her peers and showed signs of catching up with them educationally. Not so her brother, Matt. He had acquired little social awareness, reacting instinctively to any approach. He had no awareness of cause and effect, so that he was totally unpredictable. I would have to go one step at a time with that one, I thought.

At the beginning there was a preponderance of boys, the ratio about seven to one and it remained roughly so.

The only girl to come with the first intake was a little fairylike seven-year-old creature who came dressed in ill-fitting, grubby dresses and used adult phrases and struck prematurely adult stances – surprising until one read her records. As has been the custom in parts of the country where rural customs override legal rules, Margaret came from a family where the father had considered it his duty (a phrase used as a semi-conscious excuse) to initiate his daughters into what he termed the pleasures of sex. Years later, he appeared on television in a programme dealing with such aberrations and seemed quite unmoved by public opinion and conventional thinking. On the contrary, he still professed a belief in this appalling paternal behaviour. Young Margaret was prematurely aware of the needs of men and her provocative behaviour reflected the method by which she had learned to obtain attention and, possibly, the necessities of life.

Also to join us was a seven-year-old boy whose spare time was taken up with touting for custom for his mother, (who had been prosecuted in several towns for soliciting) and lately for his two older sisters. This and his predilection for shoplifting was recorded, but it was some time before the full extent of Tim's activities became known. He was one of the few children of whom I could say that they were amoral. He had been reared in a disparate family where parenting was represented by demands, threats and punishments and where a statement or an answer were constructed towards self-excuse or, indeed, self-preservation. Truth and honesty were strangers. Somehow, Tim would have to gain a consciousness of those two principles and it was up to me to discover how this may be achieved.

A boy I was looking forward to getting to know better was autistic. Guy was a handsome child who often looked anxious, as is the way with those affected by that syndrome. My first memory of him remains clear. To accustom those coming from the infant department the following term, they attended a junior assembly in their future department. As my unit was to open after the summer holiday, the top infants were accompanied by those in the infant unit who would be shortly transferring. Guy was one of these. He was led by the hand and placed in a sitting position at the front of the school. When Howard started addressing the assembly, Guy shouted out loudly, "Cucumber sandwiches." Of course, this caused great amusement and Guy stood up and faced the audience to receive his applause. The assistant managed to sit him down again, but his foray into clownship was too much to be resisted and the whole thing was repeated several times until he had to be forcibly removed from the hall. As Guy was obviously conscious of how he could create havoc, I did not feel that he was a total slave to compulsive behaviour. On the contrary, a child with the ability to keep almost three hundred children amused must possess something worth working on. I found myself eager to start.

I had acquired a second-hand filing cabinet so that records could be kept under lock and key, for they contained facts relating to families, criminal records and mental-health details. The ongoing records which I was required to keep and which may be added to after visits by educational psychologists and after case conferences which I attended were very sensitive and could be expressed more honestly if I knew that they would only be accessible to those qualified to read them.

I felt that I could do no more to prepare the surroundings, my assistant and me, but it was with a degree of trepidation that I arrived on the first day of term and waited for the arrival of the taxis which brought the unit children from all areas of the city.

I'LL TRY

I met the taxis at the school gates and took my charges straight into the building, as they all represented unknown factors at that first encounter. I trusted that they would soon become slightly more predictable.

They all looked with appreciation and some with wonder at the welcoming, colourful room and it seemed that many of them had never believed themselves worthy of such surroundings.

They could chose where they sat to do the work required of them and keep their personal belongings in their own tip-up-top desks; such a preferential arrangement compared to tables and individual lockers which give a child no feeling of belonging in any particular space.

When snacks, marbles, conkers, sweets and other treasures had been stacked away in desks, we all gathered in the carpeted area for my first attempt at establishing order out of the chaos which had largely ruled their lives. Those coming up from the infant department were not a great problem, as they knew me vaguely and had been partially prepared by their previous headmistress with whom I had been friends for many years. When we had taught together at the ESN school we had used much the same methods and had established the same standards of discipline and behaviour.

However, I started by assuring Guy that cucumber sandwiches were not part of the class curriculum and would, therefore, not be tolerated. He fixed me with a steady gaze, into which one could read anything, but never referred to them again.

That was the only negative warning at this stage, for I wanted to create a positive, rewarding atmosphere right from the beginning, so I introduced what was to form the nucleus of their daily work. Each of them would have a record booklet into which my assistant, Anne, or I would enter comments on how well they had achieved their three tasks each day. The three headings would be 'Reading', 'English' and 'Maths' and they would be expected to complete these three tasks each day. No-one would be better or worse than anyone else; only their own effort and results would be judged against their individual capability. This obviously meant nothing much to them at the time, but gradually led to terrific efforts to obtain a 'Very Good' or even an 'Excellent'. Anne and I craftily managed to insert words which the children found difficult to read. They soon found these thoroughly readable.

I had drawn out a work plan for each child, making this first one well within their capabilities, as nothing succeeds like success. The greatest advantage of this method was that, as soon as the three required tasks were completed, the rest of the day, apart from PE, games and periods when we joined with other classes, could be devoted to 'choosing'. I could see that they could hardly believe their luck, but I had lived longer than they had and knew a few tricks of which they, luckily, were still ignorant. The choosing consisted loosely of educational, constructional activities which largely required cooperation between groups of children and which would, hopefully, foster a sociability which these children lacked. There were also tasks which contributed to the enjoyment of everybody, like tidying the room, washing paintbrushes and watering the plants. This last activity, designed to foster a caring attitude towards living things tended to be construed as an excuse to flood large areas under the window sills, until it was understood that only those who performed the tasks properly would be allowed to do so again.

When a nearby school advertised an excess of stick insects,

I took in a fish tank which the late occupants had vacated some time ago. There were privet hedges round the playing field, so fetching pieces of privet to feed the stick insects and cleaning out their home became a favourite 'constructional activity'. When the insects bred, some children wanted to take a few babies home, but a letter from parents, sanctioning this had to be provided first.

That first intake represented many diverse problems, but it was intriguing to meet the children about whom I had read in their individual files. For instance, according to the written record as well as to the many anecdotes I had heard from colleagues, Richard's behaviour was capable of disrupting not only his own class, but the whole school, yet when he came to the unit, I had to acknowledge that I had never seen such a beautiful child. His blonde hair flopped over his forehead and curled gently above his ears. The shape of his face would have inspired the most discriminating of portrait painters, while his blue eyes shone with an impression of total innocence. I discovered Richard's underlying problem only gradually. Although most of the children's records showed the assessment of their IQ's (Intelligence Quotient), Richard's did not. There could have been several reasons for this; his absence or that of the educational psychologist at a date when this assessment was scheduled, Richard's refusal to cooperate or lack of time to complete the assessment. He looked such an intelligent, cooperative child that the omission remained a puzzle for some time. Only by gradual degrees did his problem manifest itself. Because his outward appearance promised so much, it fostered the human expectation that this delightful shell held a desirable content, but rather like the last chocolate which always remains in a decorative selection box, the outward appearance was totally misleading. Richard turned out to be a creature of impulse – not because he was wayward, but because he did not possess enough intellect to connect yesterday and today, right and wrong, or cause and effect. He was in the wrong environment and needed to be where he would be educated at a much slower pace than in a conventional school. After a few months with us, a place was found for him where he thrived, albeit at his own painfully slow speed. It was the first time we experienced the hole opened within our group when one child left us, but although this necessitated a new settling period, it confirmed that we were becoming an entity, dependent on each other.

Although most of the unit children lived with their parents, there were some who, for various reasons, could not. James, who had resorted to defiling his surroundings, had been rejected by his mother, who asserted that she could not remember who was his father, so he and his sister had been taken into care. They were mixed-race children who had inherited the best in looks from both parents, with coffee-coloured skin, curly black hair and melting brown eyes. The girl was also an accomplished little actress who soon worked out what was in her best interests so that she adapted to fit into her placements and caused very little trouble. James, however, was made of different stuff. He expected the placement to adapt to him and when it did not, he relapsed into raging temper tantrums. This behaviour became more pronounced when his sister received attention for being charming – a form of behaviour which James had no idea how to emulate, so he became more entrenched in activities which assured attention being switched to him. Social services, being in the era of 'keeping families together at all costs' aggravated this situation every time they persuaded other, unsuspecting foster parents to take on the pair. Just to satisfy this tenet the sister was repeatedly torn away from where she had begun to settle, and James was thrust into a new situation on which to stamp his control. By the time that James came to me, when he was seven, he had proved untenable by three schools and numerous 'placements'. He was currently in a small children's home staffed by religious, long-suffering women who were attempting to cope with his unsavoury habits. They had been advised, when admitting to complete inability to manage James, that he was to be separated and excluded until his behaviour improved – by magic, one would assume. As expected by anyone with more experience of such children, this just exacerbated the problem, for it confirmed James' belief that he was not wanted, was worth nothing and, if he wanted to register in this world at all, he had to repeat the behaviour which he knew would bring him recognition. Having no recollection of being acceptable, of receiving praise for anything he did, all the incentives were forcing him into unacceptable behaviour.

However, children are not fools and lashings of praise for doing anything which requires very little effort is patronising and unproductive. Judging by his file, already several inches thick, James had been subject to this "Leap upon anything he does right and heap praise, approval and awards on him." He had soon seen through this, as it brought sessions of recrimination. He had shown that he was aware of how he behaved and that he was capable of conforming, therefore he was berated when he reverted, however slightly, to his previous habits.

With his obvious powers of manipulation, James had a personality not easy to modify, yet to be successful, the unit must try to fit its incumbents to the world as it is, so the following weeks required a delicacy of handling and an awareness of every nuance in this boy's behaviour. At first, as is the custom with all those in new surroundings, James spent his time summing up his contemporaries, Anne and me. He sat, with arms folded, ignoring casual encouragement to tackle his three tasks, with what could be construed as a sneer when looking with pity at the other children working. Gradually, tasks were finished, comments filled in and individual stars affixed to the "Tasks Completed" chart on the wall. Large building bricks were taken out and building began. Paints were mixed and pictures took shape. Games were enjoyed by groups. Still James sat, in glorious isolation, yet taking surreptitious glances round the room, noting how his classmates were enjoying themselves. By not doing his work, he was under the impression, at first, that he had won the battle, but it eventually dawned on him that the system had won the war.

He had the inevitable noisy temper tantrum when denied the

envied 'choosing' activities, but receiving no attention for that and being accompanied to the toilet by Anne, to fend off other habits he may have chosen to repeat, he spent the rest of the days sulking in silence.

When it was time to go home, we accompanied the children out to the taxis and showed just as much affection towards James as we did to the others, which left him with a puzzled expression as his taxi drove off.

One memorable morning, James sidled into the classroom and hung around by my desk. When I had settled the others, I waited for the overture which I sensed was a difficult approach for James. However, I was surprised when I put my arm round him, that he did not pull away from me. He stayed like that for a few minutes, then he whispered, "I'll try." This was followed by a mutual cuddle and his permission that I could make his statement our class motto. So, while James attempted his first task, tactfully watched and, where necessary supported by Anne, I found an enormous piece of bright yellow card and upon it, in huge letters, wrote "I'll try." This became our lasting motto. It summed up such a lot of what we were striving for.

A better placement for James, unencumbered by an attractive, compliant sister and with a housemaster who ran a strict but loving home, enabled this boy to become one of the best loved in the school. He had a strong personality and really flourished in his securely designed background. Some years afterwards, I was invited to visit the home during the day of James' sixteenth birthday and was met by a tall, handsome young man who was overwhelmed by the number of people who called in to see him during the day, yet eager to return to his many friends and their game of football.

One particular event which I think we shall always remember, occurred when James had been with us some time and still loved attention. Luckily, he was now satisfied with earning it by doing the acceptable things and was working well, socialising and, surprisingly, enjoying being gently teased. He had discovered a talent for clowning and, while this had to be curbed at times, it gave him the joy of being noticed. As our room was a normally sized classroom and we had few children in it, the work desks could be spread out, with those children who preferred working in isolation taking themselves into a corner. I had pushed a drawing pin into the front of each desk and omitted to tell the children that I had made 'speeding tickets' – cards with pieces of cord so that they could be hung on the drawing pins. The cards bore various messages, all related to speeding, such as "You are exceeding the speed limit, take a star" or "A star has caught you speeding, put it by your name." The delight of the children must have been heard all over the school as they fell about with laughter as cards were put, surreptitiously, on the front of desks where work was being energetically tackled. The star chart, used to record attention to work and to good manners began to fill with stars for speeding. It was not long before James had earned a 'speeding card' and was overcome with excitement. By now, the unit felt a collective satisfaction at individuals' successes and a generous feeling of joy pervaded the room. After earning several of these coveted cards, I warned James that, if he worked so hard, his brain might catch on fire. This was just the sort of picturesque imagery that appealed in the unit, but I bled the humour of it a little more. Secretly, I affixed a longish piece of cotton wool to some sticky tape and, while Anne distracted his attention, I pressed this to the back of James' curls where it stuck firmly, waving above his head. As soon as they noticed, the other children's laughter made James feel above him and, on discovering the soft cotton wool, collapsed with laughter, too. This intensified when he looked in our classroom mirror. When he could catch his breath, he asked if he could go and show the other classes how his brain had caught fire. We could tell where he had reached in his tour by the direction from where the loud laughter emanated. So, the child who had felt rejected and worthless a few short months ago now toured the school, triumphantly showing off his funny spectacle and being noticed by everyone for something he had earned legitimately.

LAW 'N' ORDURE

The yob and his mate knocked off one day
A beautiful pea-green car.
They took a cosh
To extract the dosh
And Dutch courage, picked up at a bar.

The yob looked over the panel lights,
Then grinned at his mate and said,
"I'll give her the gun,
Get up to a ton
And shoot all the lights that are red."

By the time they'd found a likely spot
They were all psyched up for the kill.
Like Bonnie and Clyde,
They crashed the door wide
And took all the cash from the till.

The police leapt out, with triumphal shout
"You were not quite as good as you thought."
So they got took away
And were jailed next day
By the magistrate sitting in court.

They lived in cells, in the warm and dry,
With clean shirts, trousers and socks
And both agreed,
"It's just what you need,
When you're used to a cardboard box."

A CHIP BUTTIE

I suppose the situation could have been predicted, human nature being what it is and young human nature tending to express itself crudely when feeling unjustly treated.

I had, for several years, been the teacher responsible for helping struggling readers who enjoyed the escape from classrooms for a few minutes each day. These children, far from feeling disadvantaged, had been the envy of their more successful classmates as they flaunted their refreshingly interesting books and games borrowed from me. My transfer to a special unit, populated by strange children from other areas of Gloucester, seemed to them a betrayal of my loyalties. Soon, they saw the unit children receiving an increased amount of help, with a teacher and an assistant present to deal with the prescribed maximum of eight children. This set-up was even more strange to them than it was to me and they dealt with strangeness as animals do: by adopting an antagonistic attitude.

The majority of the unit children were able to cope with going into the playground at playtimes and lunch breaks, but some of the more volatile pupils had to be with me all day, occupied with tasks which were as interesting as I could make them. On cold or drizzly days, this group were seen as highly favoured and this contributed, no doubt, to the deprecating comments addressed towards the unit children who did not enhance their reputation when they flew into rages as they acquired unfavourable nicknames. Inevitably, my charges complained bitterly about the situation which was hardly helping them to become integrated and to behave in an acceptable manner. So, within the unit, we formed a 'secret society'. We were not going to argue with anyone about shortcomings or inabilities. All defamatory remarks would be ignored, for we had a secret.

Each child has a talent; it may take some finding, especially in a child who has been used to being denigrated and ostracised, sometimes for years, but I hoped to uncover talents before the novelty of having a secret wore off.

After a couple of weeks, we had quite a formidable pile of individual pieces of work, secreted in the cupboard, some of it maths, writing, spelling and drawing, but also impressive pieces of simple embroidery and model making.

Anne and I stayed at school one evening and mounted these admirable samples, at least one from each child, and fixed them to the noticeboards in the corridor outside our classroom.

When the unit children arrived the next day, their faces shone and we waited with great anticipation for the school's reaction. Sure enough, there were many *Cor*s and *Wow*s and comments which made our secret most effective. Thankfully, that was the end of the name-calling, but gave rise to another problem.

Children from other classes now hung around my door, asking, "When are *we* going to have *our* turn in your unit, Miss?"

There was no answer to this, apart from retreating to the position where I would have to explain that the unit children were different from them, in that they needed to be in a smaller group. Therefore, this privilege persisted in being seen as totally unfair until much later.

The whole point of the unit was to stabilise the behaviour of each child so that he or she could be accepted by society. At teacher training college, there had been a pervading accent on finding, and even pandering to 'the needs of the child'. I remembered one incident when, on a purely observational visit to a nursery class, I had seen a boy, clutching a hammer, run across the room and hit a hapless classmate on the head with the tool. The class teacher dealt with the situation by parting them, but I still remember my puzzlement when I was censured for sympathising with the child who had been attacked. I was given to understand, by those in charge of our training, that the whole of my consideration should have been to wonder at the need of the first child to attack his fellow classmate. I should, I was told, have delved into this 'need' and tried to understand it.

I regret that I could never subscribe to the belief that the world must change to accommodate the needs of a particular individual and I firmly believed that the children in my care must be fitted to live in the world as it is. Behaviour Modification is the technical term, but perhaps the phrase from *The Water Babies* describes it better: "Do as you would be done by." And it was not long before, stretched above the blackboard was the adage "If you don't like it, don't do it." This proved to be quite useful, as minor irritations became countered with "Would you like me to do that to you?" It was not always effective, but could sometimes be the "answer which turneth away wrath".

In many of the reports from previous schools, I read that 'time-out' had been recommended. This can certainly be an effective way of allowing a child (and a harassed teacher) time to calm down, but ignores the persistence of a child to re-enter the room repeatedly and to continue a destructive disruption of the whole class. Within the normal school situation, where classes are too big and habits have become engrained, the teacher has little choice and the reaction in general tends to be based on punishment or withdrawal of privileges. This is inevitable, as numbers and the pressures of the curriculum leave very little space for consideration of appropriate handling of the seriously disruptive child. Hence a negative attitude and an oft repeated admonition to "Stop it."

By the time a child came to me, it was obvious that a request to stop whatever unsocial behaviour in which he was indulging would hardly be effective. Something else had to be substituted.

Gavin had the enviable reputation, amongst his peers, of being able to project a glob of saliva further than anyone else and, having no other obvious talents, had perfected this achievement until he had acquired the name of 'The Cobra', of which he was inordinately proud. Saliva contains various ingredients which can do damage, especially to the eyes, so that when Gavin had been the cause of several cases of conjunctivitis, the last one needing to be hospitalised, he was considered a suitable candidate for my unit.

As usual, Gavin spent the first few days summing up the situation but, being a bit of a showman, started to crave attention. When shouting at Anne or at me only brought the request that he speak instead of shouting, he resorted to his cobra routine, waiting until either of us were in range and then letting fly. To his astonishment, he was not told to stop it, but was put firmly by the sink and told to carry on spitting. Every time we passed him, we reminded him to spit, so that he was soon requesting drinks of water to cure the dryness in his mouth. On being told that, to drink water, he would have to stop spitting and that we did not want to deprive him of his favourite pastime, he became quite thoughtful and it was not long before he was leaning on the sink, looking decidedly bored. He then informed us that he had finished spitting and was allowed to go back to his work, with the warning that should he chose to spit again, he would be stationed by the sink for even longer next time. A simple solution but, thankfully, it worked.

Bernard was a lovely boy, in appearance like the illustrations of *Just William* of which I had been very fond when I started reading. He was bumbly, round and good-natured and for the first few days he exhibited no need to be in a special placement. He was amenable, social and reasonably hard-working, although his achievement was well below what it should have been.

He came from a rough area and I knew that his family had suffered some traumatic incidents, but Bernard appeared, at first, to have come through unscathed. His mother, his only remaining parent, had long been agoraphobic, but Bernard spoke of her quite fondly and there was obviously a great feeling of unity within the surviving members of the family.

Then, quite suddenly, for no apparent reason, Bernard became transformed. Whatever set off this drastic change must have been a trivial incident, for nobody seemed to have witnessed it, but the result was dramatic and could have been disastrous, for Bernard used his feet for attacking anyone and anything, kicking viciously at everything within his reach. Bravely advancing, I managed to remove his shoes and put them high up on a shelf in the cupboard. Anne had removed the other children to a safe distance. The kicking continued for a while, but subsided as Bernard's feet became sore from kicking the furniture. He sobbed for a while, but refused to be comforted or cuddled, lying exhausted until playtime, when he demanded his shoes. I had to reply that I could not return them as he used them as weapons to hurt people and he accepted that, sitting on the doorstep all playtime. At lunchtime he went into the dining room, but after he had eaten, I could not find him anywhere. As he had such a good relationship with his mother, I deduced that he would make for home, which was not far away. Sure enough, as I drove along the first road, I saw a lonely little figure walking along the grass verge, shoulders heaving with sobs. As I drew level with him and opened the door next to him, I invited him to take a ride back with me to school.

"What, in your car?" he questioned in amazement.

"Yes, because the ground must be hurting through just socks."

"I don't care," he asserted.

"No, but I care," I told him.

This seemed to puzzle him, but he got into the car and, with a huge sigh, sank down low into the seat beside me. When we got back to school, he was disinclined to get out of the car, but addressed me,

"You won't tell our mum, will you, Miss?"

"Not if you don't want me to and as long as you have given up kicking."

"I have," he promised. "And thank you for the lift," he added, in the manner of one adult friend to another.

As soon as I could, I tried to visit the homes of my charges, but this was difficult with no working time allotted to so innovative an activity. Bernard's house was almost on my route home, so I made it one of the first visits. His mother had refused to let anyone in until the educational psychologist in charge of Bernard's placement had managed to cross the threshold. He often managed to be invited into situations where others had been repeatedly denied, for he was a big man, with a big heart and was an excellent listener. However, I felt honoured to be only the second visitor to be welcomed by a woman who had been a recluse for many years. I braved the inevitable cup of tea and the embarrassed silence which accompanied it at first. Then, as if a dam had broken, Bernard's mother broke into the most embarrassing praise of our school and especially the unit that we had ever heard. I learnt that Bernard, right from the beginning, had been decidedly reluctant to go to school, giving as one of his excuses a fear that his mother might disappear while he was away. Even when he had attended his previous school, he often did not stay long, disappearing off home at any opportunity. Social workers had had the unenviable job of extracting him from under his bed, being resisted and kicked for their pains.

Now, Bernard's mother assured me, her son loved coming to school and dreaded the holidays.

Later, we were able to arrange stints at summer-school activity holidays for him, but for the present the unit seemed to be performing an invaluable service.

Perhaps we had become a little too indispensable, for soon afterwards, in the middle of one morning, the secretary came into the room and informed me that there was an urgent phone call for me and the caller could not wait. She remained with my class while, with trepidation, I went to her office. To my initial relief and then my surprise, Bernard's mother had left her house and found a phone box so that she could speak to me. The implications of her foray into the outside world were a matter for rejoicing, but her message, while sad, remains with me as a source of great amusement.

"Oh, Mrs Dowding, I thought you'd like to know. I just can't get on with me new teeth. They rattles around and hurts me mouth. I just can't get on wiv them. I can only suck at a chip buttie."

I felt flattered by this vote of confidence and resolved to build on it.

This was not to be, as not long afterwards a teenage trainee social worker was assigned to this family and, in one disastrous visit, cancelled the trust that had begun to build up between Bernard's mother and 'the authorities'. She became again a complete agoraphobic, having been pushed too far by a young person without the training or the natural ability to deal effectively with her. However, this accentuated an aspect which we had not foreseen and allowed it to be corrected before such progress could again be undermined.

In future, social services were required to take advice from the unit staff before attempting contact with the families involved. This proved to be a two-way benefit, as it gave us the ability to consult each other on many occasions and always to the benefit of a child who was, after all, our mutual concern.

THE TURKEY DIARY

March
I'm just a little fluffy chick. I'm still quite small and damp.
I've hatched out from a turkey's egg kept underneath a lamp.

April
We run around and fight for food, pecking one another.
We have no manners for, you see, we haven't got a mother.

May
My mates do lots of silly things, like hang themselves on wire.
Suicide would seem their aim, their feverish desire.

June
The sun is hot, the air is still, a dust bath pure delight,
But goodness knows why all of us are shut in sheds at night.

July
Last night we found the reason why. While perching in our beds
A wily fox came creeping in and bit off twenty heads.

August
A good year's harvest, so they say; hard work to night from morn.
It's heaven for us growing birds, with barns so full of corn.

September
Today some great big lorries came and loaded up my mates –
The squawking was quite tragic as they drove off through the
    gates.

October

It's very odd, now I'm alone. My mates are here no more.
They're perching in another place called Tesco's frozen store.

November

Competition – I have none. Of all I am the king.
I strut my stuff. I'm full of pride. I fear not anything.

December

Today I heard the farmer say, (I thought it was in jest),
"Stoke up the oven ready, dear. I'm glad I kept the best."
Here comes the ruddy farmer now. Oh God, he's got a knife!
Oh, bubble, bubble, toil and trouble, he's going to take my

IF YOU CAN'T BEAT THEM . . .

One problem we knew we would have to face was the attitude of parents when it was suggested that a child could benefit from coming to our unit. What had to be taken into consideration was that, quite possibly, complaints from schools and neighbours had forced many parents into adopting a defensive attitude. This is only natural, when the world seems to be 'against' their offspring. When an official-sounding educational psychologist is introduced to the case, a mental panic can set in.

With all the pressures on education in general and especially upon the overcrowded duties of the staff in a school it is, unfortunately, time with parents which often takes a back seat.

Mothers, particularly, feel that they must wait for a parents' evening to approach their child's teacher, despite having worries that could be quickly sorted out to the benefit of the child and which could prevent further deterioration in that child's scholastic progress. More importantly, a child's behaviour in school can become unsociable, disruptive or both with no apparent reason when contact between home and school may promptly have discovered an underlying cause. An increased level of understanding at a crucial time could have helped to prevent the escalation of a harrowing situation.

Many parents of my proposed charges already felt antagonistic towards the education system in general and any suggestion that a child was again to be singled out, for whatever purpose, immediately aroused suspicion and a reluctance to cooperate. This we met to varying degrees. Our first task was to settle the graduates from the infant unit into their new surroundings, which was comparatively easy, as the help offered by this type of education was already appreciated by those children and their parents alike. The children from other schools were a different matter. Those living locally had heard of the infant unit and of how the children there had been accepted and had greatly benefited, but in other areas, the words 'Special Unit' conjured up visions of yet more adverse criticism of their child and, by reflection, of them as parents.

It was sad to hear that some children, sadly in need of special support and the expertise that we could offer were denied this because the parents summarily dismissed the whole idea straight away. The educational psychologists found this upsetting and distressing, but, from a parent's angle I could understand this. After all, the idea of special units was a new one and even the name could sound terrifying. What was this alien-sounding provision into which the so-called experts wanted to plant their child? Looking at it from their point of view, I could fully understand their reticence to consider such a move. It was even to be admired in a parent who cared about the welfare of their child.

There was only one answer. Rather than have a child-led admission procedure, we would make it parent-led. Fathers and mothers, or most usually mothers, could come and spend some time with us and we would do our best to include them in understanding our methods and the reasons for our actions. Anne and I were a little nervous at first and afraid that we would be put on the defensive, but the visitors were, without exception, interested and non-judgemental. They approved of the friendly surroundings and of the way that the children chatted to them quite openly and the experiment seemed to have worked.

It worked almost too well, as all those who came for a visit became quite militant in their demands that their child should be offered a place in the unit and offered a place immediately. Thereafter, great consideration had to be given to which children could benefit most from this type of education before hopes were raised amongst the parents. A huge advantage ensued from these initial visits. As the parents had, in effect, pressed for a placement it set the tone for cooperation in our methods and procedures. There was an awareness that to be offered a place in the unit was a privilege and that for this to continue there needed to be support at home.

I had already met Guy's mother. She was a pretty, well-spoken woman who obviously adored her two boys, of whom Guy was the oldest. She had accepted that, being autistic, Guy was a little different from the general population, but desperately wanted him to be able to fit into society and eventually into a job which would support him financially. This, I assured her, was our aim for every one of our charges and we would do our level best for Guy. This was not difficult as he was an appealing boy who increasingly exhibited his considerably superior intelligence.

It is an unfortunate fact that, once a label has been attached to a child, all sorts of assumptions are made, the most damaging one being that *all* the traits attached to that category apply to that child. What is more, it is often assumed that those indications must be present in their most severe form.

No wonder that educationalists are so reluctant to diagnose specific learning difficulties, for such a pronouncement could turn out to be a lifetime handicap.

In the unit, I was determined that we would be dealing with little human beings, all different, but all with the potential to fit into the world as they found it. No matter what learning or behavioural difficulties they exhibited, the aim would not be to accentuate these, but to encourage behaviour which was publicly accepted as normal. Guy's mother welcomed this attitude, as her son's behaviour could have been seen as charming if a little bizarre, when he was small, but now that he was bigger and beginning to enjoy an audience, autism was taking over the lives of the whole immediate and extended family. She agreed that their expectations of him must change.

Behaviour which was socially unacceptable would be

corrected and he would gradually be made to accept social approaches, an attribute which is very difficult for most autistic children to acquire.

The chance to make Guy not only receptive to, but also appreciative of physical human contact came sooner than expected. For once, it was atrocious weather which aided rather than hindering progress. Guy's mother had warned us that he was absolutely terrified of thunder and lightning; so much so, that she had made arrangements to leave her job and rush to his school to try to comfort him, but no matter how it was explained to him that there was nothing to be frightened of, the terror still remained.

The term was only a few days old when the large picture windows of our classroom became dark grey as thunderclouds rolled towards us. When close to Guy, I remarked to Anne that I hoped there was not going to be a thunderstorm as I was absolutely terrified of the noise and of the flashing lights. We knew each other's ways well enough for her to commiserate rather than blindly to reassure. At the first flash of lightning, I made sure that I was beside Guy and ready to clasp him and appear to share his fear as the initial roll of thunder echoed around us. At first, Guy was, obviously, too terrified to speak, but as I cuddled him tightly he gradually became less tense. He relaxed still more when Anne remarked, "It's nice to see someone comforting Mrs Dowding. She doesn't like thunderstorms, you know."

I felt Guy's attitude swell from sheer terror to inordinate pride. He actually flung his arms round my neck and told me that he would stay with me until the thunder had gone. By the time his mother, as promised, had reached the school, she was met by a very proud son who bragged about looking after his teacher because, he said with a hint of disdain, "She's frightened of thunder storms."

If ever there were a better reason for citing the saying "If you can't beat them", join them, I cannot imagine it.

Guy went on to become one of our greatest successes,

sometimes by accident. I am extremely allergic to onions and our excellent chief school cook always made me a special portion devoid of onions if they were present in the main meal. Guy had replaced his constant seeking of attention for being different, and had now discovered that he gained far more by fostering what he observed to be normal in others. He was intrigued by the idea that a food could actually do harm and persuaded the cook that he could not tolerate onions, either. He completely won over the whole kitchen staff by fixing them with his big brown eyes and asking most politely, if it would be too much trouble to make him meals without onions, too. How could they resist such an appealing request?

He said nothing about this at home, yet about two weeks later his mother came to see me, delighted with the progress that Guy had made lately. He was getting on with his younger brother better, sleeping undisturbed throughout the night and nowhere near as fussy with his food.

However, he had acquired an aversion to junk food. Instead of relishing a trip to McDonald's as a reward for suffering a shopping trip, he demanded what he called "a proper meal where I can see what I'm eating". The only other erstwhile favourite meal which he now resolutely refused to touch was the hotpot she usually made for Saturday's dinner. His behaviour had shown such improvement and he had become so much calmer that she overlooked these seemingly adverse changes. I had been aware for years of how even the proximity of onions affected me, but Guy had never shown an allergic reaction. By continuing a diet which was scrupulously free of onions, however, Guy's tense behaviour gradually disappeared and while autistic traits remained, we dealt with them with increased ease.

Guy went on to be transferred gradually to normal classes until he left us at eleven. I was flattered that I was the first person to hear from his mother after she had opened the envelope and found that Guy had been offered a place in a grammar school. I was happy to join her in her tears.

This incident made me very aware of how items of diet can affect behaviour, yet this was before the effect of food dyes and other additives had been studied. The children who came to us were, because of their often obstructive behaviour the ones who ate the most restrictive diet, sometimes having chosen to live on convenience snacks or strictly one type of food, such as chocolate or cheese. For a growing child this could prove disastrous physically as well as for their mental potential.

There was a small room off the main dining room where we set up a family-style dinner time. Anne and I sat round the table with the children, except when one of us was on main-room dinner duty and we set the expectations for every child. No-one was allowed to refuse an item because they said that they did not like it. They were expected to try a minute portion and, if their opinion remained the same, they would not have to eat that particular thing for about a month, after which they were expected to try a really tiny piece again. It was quite surprising how many children found a previously refused food acceptable on only the first tasting, but there was never any pressure to eat a normal portion of anything they really could not stand, or, of course anything to which they had an adverse reaction. Added to this, we had constant reminders in posters and informal lessons of how important different groups of food are to our bodies. Some children had become distressed by the furore at home which ensued from their constant food refusals and were in danger of viewing all food as something to be avoided, but by open discussion of the properties of food groups, they mostly managed to accept a more balanced diet. About this time, I read of an experiment with quite young children. The different categories were freely available to them all day. At first, a limited selection of favourite foods were chosen and eaten in constant snacks, but the variety gradually increased and the frequency of eating gradually decreased until most children stopped their other activities to eat bigger portions at a time and at fairly regular intervals. The most surprising thing was that they all ended up, after a few weeks, by selecting for themselves what is considered to be a balanced diet. They made choices from the groups of food, thereby including all the ingredients they needed. A lesson, I felt, for us. We were dealing with stressed children and anything which rendered their lives calmer could only be for the good.

...JOIN THEM

After just over a year of devoted service to our unit, Anne moved on to gain further experience and we were left, at short notice, to find another assistant. In this instance, qualifications were not the main requirement for such a position; interaction between children and the chosen adult had to be assessed, and the only way I could see of doing this was to invite all seemingly suitable applicants to spend a half-day with us. During this time, I could observe how perceptive the adult was and who could, therefore, be understanding of an individual child's difficulties. Of even more consequence, knowing the children as I now did, their response to each applicant would be of vital and decisive importance.

Six ladies all living reasonably locally, were allotted a morning or an afternoon. As each arrived, I somewhat cruelly only asked them to make themselves at home and to help any child they considered to be floundering. A basic requirement of an assistant in such a unit is that she must be able to think for herself, while taking 'the tone, the ambience' from the teacher.

I watched the eagerness of two visitors wane rapidly when they were unable to adapt to a situation where they had received no specific instruction. They showed no initiative. A plea for guidance would have shown a little, but they were ready to quit after a couple of hours. Two applicants were confident in their ability to 'handle' children, one even quoting that she knew exactly how to deal with all children, of all ages, as she had brought up two of her own and, she assured me, "They can't be all that different." Little did she know.

I was becoming increasingly despondent when the fifth visitor proved such a walkover that the children were issuing instructions to her and she was obeying them blindly. Before one of them persuaded her to do herself a potentially fatal injury, I sent her to the staffroom to put the kettle on.

Only one more to go and I was beginning to envisage starting the next term without an assistant. Then, on the last morning, Pam came. She had already brought up her family and decided to take teacher training, for which she applied. She received the news that she was accepted for the following year at the same time as she found that she was pregnant again. Pam compromised and took the excellent local nursery nurses course and sailed through it easily. The vacancy in the unit occurred just as she was looking for her first job in education.

What a difference! Within a few minutes, Pam was surrounded by children who accepted her request that she attend to one at a time and everywhere she went in the room there remained a happy, calm atmosphere. At the same time, I sensed that she was taking her cue from how I treated each child.

Pam had applied for other posts and had interviews arranged. Howard and I had a quick conversation as soon as she had left the school, then I called at her house on my way home to offer her the post – and that is how we secured a treasure not only for the unit but for the school as a whole.

Pam was a little unclear about her role, but I did not want to be too specific, as I felt that having to deal with two different people during the day would preserve a broader view for the children than if they had a person and an identical shadow. While, obviously, expected standards of behaviour and procedures were set by me and would never vary, it was valuable for them to see that two people can have differences of opinions which were settled amicably. They also had the benefit of the natural talents of two of us. I had never achieved the ability to help children to make music, although I had always sought to lead them into the appreciation of beautiful sound. Pam had a lovely voice and was a member of one of the leading choirs in the city, so she introduced a new skill into the school.

After about a month, Pam said, in a tone of joyful discovery, "I know what my role is. It's to watch your back."

Nicely put, as much for occasional safety as for the purposes of presenting a united front.

It was as well that I had such an assistant by the time that Kenneth was brought to my attention. I had heard of him for some time, as he lived not far away from me and I had been regaled with tales of Kenneth by very many neighbours. I would not have believed that such a small person could wreak such havoc over such a wide area if so many people had not told the same tale. He was reputed to have temper tantrums which went on for hours and with which his parents were seemingly unable to deal. He could not be left on his own without the fear of what he might do. He was a master of demolition.

I was not surprised when his name appeared on a file handed to me by one of the educational psychologists. Neither he nor the substantial file told me much more than I knew already. The psychologist was very honest, pointing out that Kenneth's presence in the unit could be curtailed at any time and that it looked as if it could only be a staging post, acting as an assessment for what ought to come next. I love a challenge, but if I had known what was to come, my heart would have quailed.

However, anyone who, at the age of seven can swear for several minutes without repeating himself and who has beaten two intelligent parents and four grandparents into total submission must have something worth working on.

New members were to be fed in gradually, so that each new arrival entered a reasonably calm, structured unit, so Kenneth came to us when we were not yet up to full strength.

As usual, for the first couple of days he assessed his position, darting eyes around the room like a python looking for its next unsuspecting meal. I could feel the vibes as I went past him – the suppressed energy. When it was in imminent danger of bursting forth, I flung myself on the floor and started screaming. Pam, party to this pre-planned fiasco, could scarcely keep her face straight. It was interesting to note that the 'old-timers' who had been with us for some time just glanced down and then went on with their work. I like to think that they knew what I was doing rather than suspecting my sanity. After all, it was only a few days since Pam and I had broken into a dual sand dance for no apparent reason but much to the amusement of the whole unit children. Many of them had experienced a lot of unhappiness in their lives and it was part of our job to redress the balance as much as we could.

After a few minutes of looking extremely puzzled, eventually his curiosity overcoming him Kenneth enquired, "Hey, Mrs Hunt. What's she doing?"

Pam: "Never you mind. Get on with your work."

After a while, Kenneth: "How's anyone supposed to get on with their work with that noise going on?"

Pam: "I know, it's dreadful, isn't it?"

Here I had to turn away from the class, as I was laughing so much and hoping that my heaving shoulders would convincingly simulate temper.

Kenneth: "Well, what's she doing, anyway?"

Pam: "She's having a temper tantrum."

Kenneth: "Well, she don't half look daft."

Pam: "I know, but that's what people look and sound like when they're in a temper."

Kenneth: "I don't like her like that."

At which point he received no answer, so that his last comment would register.

I managed to wipe the tears of laughter from my face and emit several large sighs before resuming a teacher's place in the unit. Oddly enough, we never saw a full-blown Kenneth temper tantrum. He had condemned them with his own mouth.

This still left free rein for Kenneth's imaginative mind. One could almost read his frustration while he tried to think of some trick which would conquer this strange new authority.

It was not long before he strode into the room one morning and announced, in a voice like that of a town crier, "I ain't going to do no work today."

The grammar was traditional Gloucester, the attitude was traditional Kenneth and required an inventive response. He was spoiling for a fight; waiting to be contradicted as he had been for as long as he could remember. Quick thinking had to break the habit.

I had been sharpening pencils as the children came in, so I smiled and said, "That's great. I found a magic pencil in the box this morning. It can grant just one wish, so you are the lucky one, Kenneth. You can have the whole day without doing any work."

This was obviously a shock for him, but he brazened it out, even when I cleared a large space in the middle of the floor and set in the middle of it a lone chair. I cheerfully sat him upon this and told him that he now had his wish to do nothing all day.

Pam and I then went about our usual daily duties of helping each child to finish their three allotted tasks. I kept a surreptitious eye on Kenneth whose mien stayed triumphant for longer than I had believed it would before boredom gradually set in.

"I wouldn't mind doing a bit of work," he informed us. "Not much, mind," he added hastily in case we should think that he had submitted to authority.

"Sorry, the magic has worked and I don't think it can be undone," I replied.

This gave him food for thought for a while, but when he started trying to distract the attention of the other children he only got dismissive replies. They were used to working with concentration to get their three daily tasks finished as soon as possible, with the hope of receiving excellent comments in their booklets which they took home each weekend.

Kenneth went very quiet for quite a long time, but while I was sitting with my back to him and attending to Guy, I felt a little hand on my shoulder followed by a very wet face, while a small voice in my ear said, "Please can you take away the magic? I'm ever so bored."

He was much too macho to submit to a comforting cuddle, but was content when we found the 'magic' pencil and banished it to the highest shelf in the cupboard.

After so many years of practice it was inevitable that Kenneth would be a master inventor of ideas with which to disrupt any situation in which he found himself. During a period of his compliance it was like experiencing the oppressive calm which precedes a thunderstorm. One could almost sense the build-up in his volcano.

I was not aware of what started the argument between him and Richard until both of them started shouting at each other. Richard soon sensibly gave up, recognising when he was beaten in the volume department, which incensed Kenneth. He could not bear to be ignored, so he stood on a chair to continue his diatribe.

Eventually, Richard looked up at him and instructed, with a surprising knowledge of history, "Oh, shut up. You sound just like Hitler."

Without pausing for breath, Kenneth flung his arms in the air and confidently declaimed,

"I'm not Hitler. I'm GOD."

If there is any answer to this, I have never found it. I did repeat the incident to the local vicar at his next visit, but he, having a wicked sense of humour, suggested I challenge Kenneth to prove it.

No fear. He created enough havoc with a small human's powers. Who knows what may have happened if he had learnt superhuman tricks?

50 MILLION SMACKERS

Come on, me brave lads, there's a job to be done.
    It's no time for lying in bed.
There's a fortune in notes just waiting for us –
    Stacked up in Securitas' shed.

Tom, you nick a van and make sure that it's big
    Enough to take millions away.
We don't want it stacked from axle to roof,
    And some left at the end of the day.

Dick, you get a car and make it a fast
    One for getting away at a lick,
For after we've tied up the staff with some string
    We shall have to vamoose pretty quick.

The thought of that lolly in our sticky mitts
    Makes me mouth water, makes me palms sweat –
The only conundrum remaining to solve
    I've not got me head around yet.

With folks so suspicious and lacking in trust
    And us having more than they thought,
It could be a mountain of waste paper, lads,
    For if we try to spend it, we're caught.

LOVE ME, LOVE MY PARENTS

Although our main aim must be to enable each child to thrive within an ordinary class, many of our intake had shown an originality which did not easily fit into the classroom. It was difficult to temper talents into an acceptable form without the danger of discouraging or even obliterating natural attributes.

Kenneth's parents and grandparents were all competent people, successful in their different fields and I suspected that Kenneth felt that he had to be perfect in order to belong. His little sister was a sweet little thing who did not need to seek approval. I surmised that his behaviour stemmed from frustration at not knowing how to be accepted. This was a great mistake on his part, as his family loved him, despite the almost constant disruption and complaints about his exploits. They were most anxious to know how to help him, but first he had to learn to accept himself without needing to be perfect.

Pam and I were continually showing affection to all the children. This not only made us approachable, but, hopefully made up for the loving acceptance which many of them had never yet experienced – at home or at school. Gradually, each one came to realise that he or she could come to either of us with any problem or confidence, secure in the knowledge that it would be dealt with sympathetically and, if admissible, confidentially. The only exception was, predictably, Kenneth. He resolutely refused to acknowledge that he was in any way incompetent, but Pam and I made a point of asking each other for help or of needing to look up answers in books, while making sure that Kenneth observed this. Then, one day, like the first ray of sunshine after black clouds have parted, Kenneth asked me, "How do you spell 'house'?"

I pretended to think about it, then noting that Pam had heard, I said, "I'm not sure. It begins with a 'h', I think. Ask Mrs Hunt if she knows."

Kenneth went over to Pam and told her, in a tone of utter disgust, "Mrs Dowding doesn't even know how to spell 'house', and she's supposed to be a teacher!"

"Nobody knows *everything*," responded Pam, "but I'm sure she'll help you to find out."

This deflated Kenneth's superiority, somewhat, but an invitation to accompany me to ask Mr Watts, the headmaster, boosted it again.

With a large wink from behind Kenneth, I asked Howard if he knew how to spell 'house'. He looked suitably puzzled for a while, then he said, "I don't need to know everything and I'm never absolutely certain how to spell some words, but you can ask my secretary to look it up for you. She types all my letters for me and looks up difficult words in a dictionary."

Kenneth had now entered a world he had not known existed. A headmaster admitted, quite cheerfully, that he did not know everything. He was rather dazed as I took him through the open door and into the room where the secretary had heard the current conversation. She welcomed him in and, in a businesslike fashion, asked him what he wished her to look up.

Although suffering from shock, Kenneth managed to tell her his request and she helped him to find the appropriate page, even typing out the word for him. He returned to the classroom, clutching his precious piece of paper and obviously deep in thought.

This may appear to have been a waste of time, an unnecessary diversion from drumming in the 'three Rs', but it is the latter which has led to many children missing out some humane element just when they were in desperate need. It solved a problem for one struggling child for evermore and made him able to ask for help when he needed it, although it did a disfavour to the reputation of teachers and headmasters when word spread that we could not spell a simple word like 'house'.

All this time while we were finding Kenneth increasingly biddable, his behaviour at home did not improve. His parents came to see me in desperation, reporting that he would not get up in the mornings and there was a struggle to try to dress him and get him to eat some breakfast before the taxi arrived to bring him to school. His father was repeatedly late for work, as he had to extract Kenneth forcibly from his bed, or from under it, hold him while his mother applied his clothes and then carry him, struggling, downstairs where he either refused to eat his breakfast or spread it in runny streaks, across the kitchen before being thrust into the waiting taxi.

This was one of the easiest problems to solve. Trusting that the exhausted parents would cooperate, I asked them to put Kenneth's school clothes into a bag which they could give to the taxi driver the next morning, extract their son from bed and put him, just as he was, into the taxi. Mother suggested sending a snack for him to eat at break time so that he would not remain hungry until dinner time, but that would weaken the lesson which, I hoped would only need to be taught once.

That evening, I warned the excellent taxi driver who by now was accustomed to the vagaries of his passengers, but made no mention of the change in routine to Kenneth.

The next morning, a dejected little figure in stripy blue-and-white pyjamas and embarrassing slippers with rabbits nodding on their toes came across the playground carrying a bulging plastic bag. We made no concessions for him, for it was a beautifully warm summer day. He had to wait until the doors opened and everyone joined their classes. I think the other children were too stunned to see someone turn up in their pyjamas to laugh at him. He retired to the store cupboard to get dressed and emerged looking quite sheepish – a first for Kenneth. We were right; that particular lesson never had to be repeated.

This was another incident which strengthened my belief that these children had had adverse criticism until they had ceased to hear it or had so come to expect it that it meant nothing to them. They had never found out the natural consequences of their actions or had to take personal responsibility for them.

One seven-year-old came to us with the reputation of repeatedly biting. According to the records from his previous schools he had entered the reception class with an unenviable reputation from the playgroup he had attended for a while. At the age of three he was already an outcast, for he seemed to have a compulsion to bite anyone who came within range. The playgroup staff had, understandably, refused to keep him with other children whose parents were threatening to take legal steps against them because of the frequent bite marks observed upon their children. Soon, children at three other schools where he had been placed became terrified of him and the more they shied away from him, the more he resorted to the only thing that seemed to bring him the attention he sought – biting.

Excluded from conventional education, he was granted the services of a home tutor for a few hours a week, but it was not long before she refused to spend time with a child who bit her if even slightly displeased.

Kyle was to be in our unit as a 'holding place' while the authorities tried to find a more permanent place for him. The idea was that with two adults in the room we could keep him away from the other children. This was extremely difficult, as it cut the amount of time we could spend in helping the others and meant that either Pam or I had to be with him throughout the day – playtimes and lunch breaks included.

He could not be foisted onto any of the other teachers, so we had to take him with us on our previously planned trip to see the animals beyond Prinknash Abbey. Pam entered the enclosure first, paying for us all and buying some bags of corn so that the children could feed the birds and the goats. With Kyle's hand grasped firmly in mine, we entered last. I was unaware that Canada geese could move so quickly or be so terrifyingly ferocious but one, lurking by the entrance, instantly launched itself at Kyle and bit him quite hard on his arm. I have never seen a child so shocked. He went quite pale. Pam and I could not resist accentuating the lesson and told him that creatures knew who was unkind and the goose had taught him a lesson. We did not really believe it, but Kyle did. For the rest of the visit he kept me between him and any stray Canada goose and for the rest of his stay with us he never bit anyone again.

There was invariably humour within the unit, but sometimes it emanated from outside. David was a very intelligent boy, registering an IQ well within the top ten per cent of the population. After meeting his parents, a nice but very ordinary couple, I looked in David s notes to see if he had been adopted, but seeing no sign of that I was left to wonder at the ability of advantageous genes to skip generations.

Both parents came to me to confess that they were quite willing to discipline David, because they had been told (by whom? I wondered) that that was all he needed. Their immediate problem was that they did not understand when David needed to be disciplined and what they should do about it.

David's father was a very large (in all directions) lorry driver, so 'timeout' was by far the safest advice, so I told them to judge David's need for discipline by whether he was annoying them. If he was doing so or disrupting the rest of the family, he should be removed from them, possibly to his bedroom, assured that they would miss him and left on his own so that he and they could cool down.

"How can we do that?" they asked.

I was a little taken aback by the naivety of the question and said, partly in jest, "Just go downstairs and have a double whiskey!"

It was several weeks later when David's parents came to

school and were most effusive in their thanks. They reported that they had followed my instructions almost to the letter, but feared that the idea would not work.

"Why were you doubtful?" I asked.

"Well," said large, beaming father, "David didn't like missing any TV when we put him in his room but we didn't have any whiskey in the house. We only had beer and the wife doesn't like beer, but she had a few sips of mine and the whole thing seems to have done the trick."

One problem solved, I thought, but David's mother came into the school again quite soon after and was quite distressed. Her complaint went like this: "I took our David into town. I don't like taking him, becaused he lags behind all the time, but he needed new shoes and you can't get those on spec, can you? We'd been to lots of shops and David wouldn't try on anything that he said wasn't 'in', so I was already hot and bothered. Then we were going down the main road and he was lagging behind me, as usual and all the drivers started looking at me – I thought they were flirting with me until I saw they were laughing." Her appearance hardly confirmed the prospect of flirting, but she continued: "I looked behind me, at our David and he was making one and two-fingered salutes at all the drivers."

I could not gather whether her distress was caused by disappointment that she had not personally received flattering attention or whether it stemmed from David's embarrassing gestures, but I did know that it took a lot of effort to save my laughter until she had gone. I gave David challenging tasks and got his standard of work up to quite an advanced level. His mental stimulus now came from hard work at school so that he was far more willing to relax at home, becoming acceptably amenable. As with all our unit children, as soon as possible we gradually integrated him into other classes until he did not need us any more. His parents were astounded but delighted when he won a place at a grammar school where he was reported to be doing very well.

As I had worked at the school for some years before the unit opened, the staff considered me to be one of them and we worked amicably together as we had when I had extracted children who needed a boost with their reading. Pam's talent was used for music with other classes and our children joined activities in which they showed an interest. One teacher was an accomplished artist and model maker and several from the unit benefited from his influence. Another was an excellent leader at outdoor games and Mark, especially, became a bit of a star because of his expertise.

Mark was of mixed parentage, his mother and he having had to escape a vicious regime where his father had been incarcerated. Nothing had been heard of his father for months and then years, until it had to be assumed that he had, like so many others, met a cruel death.

Understandably, Mark was a very disturbed boy. His mother did her best, but his grandmother, in whose house they lived, tended to argue with her over bringing up Mark. He grew to be very large for his age and was one of the handsomest boys in the school. His first day was memorable.

As our method of allowing visits from parents first worked so well, we had kept to it. This had the added advantage of each child coming to us unaccompanied by anxious parents. It rather resembled jumping in at the deep end, but avoided them associating the unit with parental angst.

I had heard of Mark and read the copious notes in his file. He had performed various dastardly tricks in two schools, but when he threatened to kill his headmaster by impaling him on a fence post, it was considered time to do something more than a simple transfer. Hence admittance to the special unit, even if it had to be of a short duration.

Mark was thrust into the room by a social worker who announced, "This is Mark. You're expecting him." before shutting the door behind him and scuttling off the premises.

I was deeply occupied with another child who could not be left immediately, but Pam stepped into the breach admirably.

"Oh, I'm so glad you've come, Mark. I can't reach the high shelf in the cupboard. Could you come and get something down for me?"

It was obviously not the welcome he had envisaged, for now he was integrated immediately by a crafty assistant who had sensed just the right approach.

Through the open door of the cupboard I heard, "Oh, thank you. You came just at the right time. Now what else do you think you could do for me?"

After a few very loud, sullen noises,

"Please speak softly to me. You see, I am an old lady and if someone shouts at me I can't hear them properly."

The sullen noises changed to "What do you want me to do?"

The relationship was becoming so successful that I left it to Pam to explain the classroom systems to Mark and never ceased to wonder at how this little lady had so quickly tamed so large a boy.

This relationship flourished throughout his time at the school, even when he transferred to other classes and he found great success in athletics, thanks to our member of staff who gave him such encouragement.

A few years later we were saddened to hear of his death. Probably missing out on his epilepsy medication, he had fallen from a high-speed train and had been killed. We thought we could do nothing for his distraught mother, but she made a special journey to tell us that her beloved only son had found a time of peace and happiness with us. We felt very humbled.

THE POSITIVE APPROACH

We had to find something to take the place of "No", of "Stop it" and of the myriad of threats, real and assumed with which the unit children had been assailed for years. An unfailingly positive attitude had to be constructed so that each child could succeed.

A large chart took pride of place at the front of the room, with individual names down the left side. As each term progressed, the rows of stars grew while good work and cooperative behaviour were noted. The children became very proud of this chart, pointing it out to any visitor, confident that each star represented their own, personal effort.

One mistake that I was determined not to copy was the act of taking away these hard-earned points because of bouts of bad behaviour. Stars had been earned and deserved a permanent record, not persistent anxiety that they could be taken away again, thereby negating previous effort. Accolades earned for positive progress lose all their positive encouragement if they are in danger of disappearing because of a little regression.

A record of a child's current number of stars was noted on the booklet he or she took home each weekend, so forming another audience for a week's work. At first, the booklets were very slim, having a page for each day and only recording a week's work. This enabled each child to start afresh each Monday, with a chance to improve on last week's record, but we were later able to enlarge the pages to include whole months and then terms, as children became more proud of their achievements.

Each day had four headings: English, Maths, Science and Constructional Activities. The last heading applied to a chosen activity which was enjoyed only after the other three had been satisfactorily completed, thereby giving an incentive to work hard and with concentration on the day's essential requirements. Each evening, I wrote a note of what the next day's first tasks were to be. These were almost invariably different for each child, as they all worked at their own pace and to their own capabilities. If they were compared at all it was with their own past achievements, although there was often a race to see who would complete the three tasks first and thereby obtain the right to chose a favoured occupation, such as making a house for the hamster or accompanying Pam to get food for the stick insects.

In most respects, our structure followed the integrated day, a necessary adaptation as none of our children were at the same stage of learning at any one time, unless one counted the preponderance of children who came to us with very little or even no scholastic achievement. There were obviously times when the feeling of belonging to a class could be fostered; times of poetry, music and stories, the latter often followed by drama. *The Three Billy Goats Gruff* was a perpetual favourite, as a dramatic follow-up involved pushing the unfortunate troll off the bridge. This climax was endlessly enjoyed, with a carefully managed stage prepared with chairs, a table and PE mats either side to receive the vanquished troll, to the accompaniment of raucous jeers and cheers.

As with very young children, my charges relished repetition of a story where they knew the end; it was thoroughly predictable and safe. So many of them were emotionally immature and had not yet learnt there were some things and people which could be relied upon.

We made sure that a speedy, efficient completion of the

required work brought its own rewards, always bearing in mind that if a child who was genuinely struggling was not succeeding, it was the fault of the adult, not of the child. Recalling my days as a desperate, dyslexic child, I knew the helpless and emotionally destructive feeling of not understanding how to do something, yet having an instinctive knowledge that it was solely because a task was not put in a way that I would find intelligible.

Bearing this in mind and having enough staff to do so, we kept a strict eye on the needs of every single child as they worked, stepping in before desperation had a chance to establish itself.

Each subject covered many things. English could be writing a record of what we had visited or explored the day before, an expedition of discovery with a record of the findings or what I consider still the foundation of a good start to writing and spelling English exercises which require the copying of a sentence and of choosing a missing word or phrase from the ones presented. Such exercises have many advantages, the main one being that children are not constantly spelling a word incorrectly, thereby reinforcing their own mistakes. This fact gave our children a confidence that they had not had before; that with care they could write every word correctly. For extra help, each one had a little spelling book into which Pam or I would write a required word provided the book was opened at the appropriate initial page although even this was difficult for some at first.

This method, with printed books and with duplicated sheets which I wrote for children with particular needs should have been foolproof, but I am ashamed to remember how it was my fault that it failed at a time when I should have known better.

Paul was a boy who had so far survived an appalling home life. I doubt whether his mother knew who was his father – he certainly did not. She and his sisters made money in the oldest profession, with his mother, between assignations, making lists for Paul. I found one of these when he was showing me how he had tidied his desk. I asked him what it was, for it did not seem to make any sense. It started, for instance, with "hair drier, 50p" and went on to list various items at what appeared to be ridiculously cheap prices. Paul became terrified that I might take the list from him and blurted out, "Don't take that. It's our Mum's and she'll kill me if I lose it."

It was a good illustration of how a child can be totally amoral, for he had no sense of illegality in openly explaining that this was his list for the next weekend, when he had to go into the city and get all these things for his mother. He explained that the prices quoted were nothing to do with shop prices, but were the amounts his mother would pay him when he had lifted the items. I knew from his notes that Paul and his nefarious activities were known to the police, but as the law stood, apart from taking him into care, which was only effected as a last resort, he would be escorted home and given a warning in front of his mother.

Later, when he knew that he could trust me not to make further trouble for him, he confessed how badly he was treated at home when his mother learnt that he had been caught while doing her bidding. He must have cut the profit margin of the visited stores by quite a percentage, as on one momentous occasion I glimpsed him, in an oversize jacket, entering the front of the largest department store in the city and later emerging from the back exit looking like the Michelin man. We did our best while he was with us, but Paul already felt that he was not wanted, having been told so many times at home, yet he longed to belong. It was an impossible situation as, perversely, living with his mother was his overwhelming desire. Until he was eleven, he was not considered in law to be responsible for his way of life. Three years later I learnt that, on his eleventh birthday he had been arrested for shoplifting. Ironically, on this occasion he had taken a pair of trousers for himself.

It was Paul who taught me to think even more deeply about individual circumstances before I came to a conclusion. We were to make one of our frequent forays to Robinswood Hill. It was a lovely morning and we planned to set off immediately after school lunch, as we had to be back in time for the taxis to pick up children who lived all over the city.

As usual, the three basic tasks were to be completed first. For the slow ones, I tailored the tasks accordingly, so that I judged each one able easily to finish by dinner time. Paul elected to leave English until last, having finished his maths and science tasks in record time. He started his page of English, being required to state which implement we used for various familiar jobs.

Having worked hard so far, I could now sense that he had suddenly become extremely tense. His reputation at his other schools had been of a recalcitrant and sometimes destructive boy who had been known to attack teachers and assistants, but this side of him had not, so far, been exhibited to us. Yet, as I watched him I saw that he only had one more sentence to write to complete his exercise I saw and heard him dramatically explode. Amongst the threats to maim and kill anyone who dared to come near him, I gathered that he was not going to do any more work.

There was only one reply to this, "Then I'm afraid that you cannot come with us this afternoon."

To my great surprise, the shouting stopped immediately and Paul bent over his work again. I could see that he had picked up his pencil again, when I was distracted by another child's needs.

Within a minute, Christopher informed me that Paul was crying. After a reassuring cuddle, Paul sobbed that he could not do the last sentence because he did not understand it.

It read, "We cut the grass with a . . . . " and in the box of words from which to choose the answers there was "lawn mower".

Suddenly, the awful truth dawned on me. I had blamed a child for not knowing what he could not possibly have known. He lived in a terraced house which opened straight from the pavement and which sported a small, paved backyard. The only grass Paul ever saw was in the city park, the school's extensive playing field or on the lower slopes of Robinswood Hill. This was all cut with huge machinery, usually a tractor with an enormous grass-cutting trailer attached. Not only did Paul not know what a lawn mower was, he had never seen one in action.

I learnt a lot that day and the lesson was firmly driven home when we were on our way that afternoon, for we passed a garden where a lawn mower had been left in the middle of a patch of grass. Several children, in ultra-kind voices pointed it out to Paul.

I apologised to him and he assured me, "That's alright, Miss. I'll know what that thing is next time."

I, too, remembered that lesson next time.

Across the playing field grew an enormous oak tree. It was remembered by the oldest inhabitants of the surrounding estate as a background to their climbing and hiding games and was preserved when the field was fenced off as the playing area for the infant and junior schools. The children currently attending the schools appreciated the great oak. It offered shade on hot days, a finishing post for competitive games and, best of all, the site of summer lessons when teachers could be persuaded to transfer classes outside.

All the unit children thought it a fantastic idea to grow an 'oak baby', a descendant of our familiar tree, so yoghurt pots were prepared with drainage holes and filled with compost that autumn. Each child looked for a particularly plump acorn which he or she planted with concentration into the pot labelled with their name. After a good watering, the pots were put into plastic bags to retain the moisture and arranged on a shelf in the stock cupboard. A few months later, each acorn had shot up and formed a tiny tree. It was time to take them home and plant them into tended plots.

All the children carefully took their little trees and envisaged the future glory of oak trees, huge witnesses to their initial efforts; all, that is, except Paul. While the others carried their trophies out towards the waiting taxis, Paul said, "They're stupid. Who wants an oak tree, anyway? They're rubbish!"

The others looked at him in astonishment and I was prepared to remonstrate with him, when I remembered how unthinking I had been over his English exercise, not considering his background and home circumstances. Hopefully, I made up for that lapse by saying to him, "Don't you really want your little tree, Paul?"

"No, I don't. It's rubbish," he confirmed, sulkily.

"If you really mean that, could I have it please? I forgot to plant an acorn for myself and I have been wishing that I had, because I'd love one in my garden. Would you mind if I had it, please?"

Paul's face lit up. It must have been a rare, or perhaps a unique occasion for him to be able to give something of his very own to someone who really wanted it. With obvious magnanimity and even a glowing blush, he presented me with his little oak tree. It is not so little now, standing at least forty feet high, with a yearly crop of its own acorns, but still it bears the name 'Paul's oak tree'.

BEWILDERING SITUATIONS
(SOME QUESTIONS WITH NO ANSWERS)

After a time, an approaching temper tantrum sounded a warning, with various manifestations, so that often the worst effects could be avoided. It was possible to deflect a child's attention away from what gave rise to stress – an occupation or the company of another child who was found to be irritating.

Standard repetitions of behaviour were never to be relied upon. This was the reason that the post was so absorbing as well as totally exhausting.

It was with a good deal of truth that, when asked about my job, I replied, "They are supposed to be maladjusted at the beginning of each term, but *I* am at the end!"

This was a jocular reply; so much so that I would have done the job for nothing, if I could have afforded to, but I did not disclose that fact to the local authority until *after* I had retired, just in case they took me at my word.

One of the biggest dilemmas we faced was a lovely little girl with flaxen hair and a delightful laugh. Helen was almost eight years old when she came to us with the reputation of never having spoken at school. Looking into her file, I saw that every teacher who had dealt with Helen had made the same observation, yet her parents had repeatedly reported that she was a dreadful chatterbox at home. Understandably, they became distressed as no-one in the educational world appeared to believe them. After three years of undergoing the stress of being told to speak, of having her peculiarity pointed out – including by her previous headmaster who exhibited her on the stage, in front of the whole school as "the silly little girl who never speaks" – my sympathies were totally with Helen. She seemed socially capable of communicating, worked well, was more than *au fait* with maths and could read fluently. The latter ability could only be assessed by requesting written answers to questions on the material she had been reading.

Before Helen came to the unit, I made sure that the other children put the non-speaking into perspective. We had a lengthy conversation on what each of us did not like doing. Some revelations were quite entertaining, but we all understood what it was like to avoid some actions, as we hated them so and how it was cruel to force someone into such actions. I could then introduce the subject of disliking to be made to speak, which they all accepted, following the previous conversation.

My little workforce became, therefore, Helen's champions, taking to task anyone who even remarked on the fact that she chose not to speak.

As was customary by now, Helen's parents came to see us and to see the unit which was to be their daughter's daily venue. I had anticipated their most urgent question. They were bound to want to know what we were going to do about Helen's aversion to speaking at school, and were slightly taken aback when I replied, "Nothing."

I considered it Helen's choice if she spoke or not and felt strongly that, with the attention gone and the need arising, Helen would speak as much as anyone else. Mother was relieved, but I sensed that father had no more faith in me than he had learnt to expect from the rest of the educational system.

I knew that there would come an occasion when to show no reaction at all was to be very difficult. Pam and the rest of the staff fully understood the situation and agreed that, hard as it was bound to be, no reaction whatever was to be shown when Helen decided to speak at school.

She became so adept at communicating without speech that, after about six months, when she loudly told Kenneth to move out of her way, only Pam and I noticed. We both found it hard not to let the tears flow, especially as total calm was so essential. Gradually, the other children noticed, but just took the change as Helen's choice and, therefore, a perfectly normal occurrence. In time she did, indeed, turn out to be the chatterbox that her parents had claimed her to be.

Some children we were almost powerless to help. Clemmy had been her mother's carer ever since she could remember. On her young shoulders rested responsibilities which a child should never have to experience. She was the only child and had missed more school time than she had attended. Understandably, she was devoid of any sense of how to behave socially, making loud demands continually, for that was the habitual behaviour of her mother, her only familiar example.

Her mother's physical disability appeared to vary tremendously, for although Clemmy was kept responding to her needs night and day for most of the time, when her mother had an urge to visit the school, a miraculous recovery would take place. This enabled her mother to transport her huge bulk from their flat so that she could voice complaints, liberally spiced with swear words, that echoed across the playing fields. She became so notorious that an audience was often in situ before she had incriminated her first victim.

We did persevere for a few months, but the situation seemed insoluble without intervention at home. Social services eventually took over, but Clemmy never did manage to obtain an education in any establishment except in the home where she continued to be browbeaten.

A case where we acted as a 'holding station' for a very sad boy only lasted for a few weeks, but was desperately needed at the time.

Nicky and his little sister had never known their father, for he had deserted them when they were babies. Their mother did her best for them, but she was young and immature with no extended family to give her support. Nicky gradually took over more and more of the responsibility of running the home and of looking after his little sister. He watched over her, taking her to and from school, so that she was there with him when they arrived home one day to find their mother's body, propped against the oven while the sickly smell of gas told its sad tale.

A kindly neighbour took the two children in, but they were greatly traumatised and would not be parted even for a minute. Social services found a placement for the little girl, but Nicky had become like a robot, with no aims and no reaction to anything or anyone. The neighbour, although worried about his state, found him to be obedient and no trouble, so opted to keep him while a placement could be found for him. He had lost everyone who had belonged to him and we were very conscious of this when we were asked to make a temporary place for him in the unit.

We did provide a structure for him to follow and as much demonstrated affection as he would allow us to give, but a residential placement was the only more permanent solution. We had all become very fond of him and were sad to see him go, especially as his future was so uncertain.

One child whom I can still see if I close my eyes, was Donald. He was a solid little boy, with round glasses which slid down his nose and had to be hoisted back frequently with his right hand while he wrote with the left. It was this handedness which gave rise to the instruction which the educational psychologist considered I needed. While he was in full flood, interjecting questions such as "How do you find his numerical quantitative concepts?" I considered how many years I had been teaching left-handers on all subjects with very little added difficulty. Then, on remembering trying to teach knitting, I had to admit that he had a relevant point.

On the first page of Donald's notes, I read, in large letters, that he exhibited bizarre behaviour.

I searched diligently for instances of this trend, but was disappointed to find nothing, so wondered how abnormal one had to be to be considered bizarre.

Then one morning, Donald entered the classroom to the

accompaniment of a loud, buzzing noise. He shuffled to his desk, staring straight ahead and stiffly sat down. He worked as hard as he always did, but walked extremely stiffly and continued making the buzzing noise. I had to tackle the latter, as the other children were complaining about it diverting their attention.

Donald informed me that, while he was moving at all, he had to make that noise, as he was a Hoover. This required inventiveness, so I told him that I completely understood and that I would oil his motor so that he would purr, quite quietly. This seemed to meet with his approval, so I mimed a good oiling and the rest of the day was accompanied by a soothing hum.

Donald was a Hoover for several days, but that seemed to have exhausted his extended personifications, as in the future he only showed his outstanding acting ability at appropriate times. I am still puzzled about the label bizarre as I have always considered it a manifestation of a child's imagination to be able to give a convincing portrayal of someone or something other than themselves. Where would Shakespeare have been without players who were blessed with that ability?

Since my teens, I had been involved in amateur dramatics. My first part was as the Virgin Mary in *Christmas in the Market Place*, a delightful play in which a travelling group of gypsies decide to act the Christmas story to the local populace. I was told that I depicted a passable portrayal of Our Lady, after I managed to retain throughout the performance the gold-painted halo fashioned by my grandmother from the brim of one of her many hats.

Learning whole pages of words was extremely difficult, for my dyslexia could find no visual pattern to stamp it on my memory, but during the rehearsals I learnt the music of the piece and could fit my contribution into the appropriate parts and hope that the producer either did not notice or did not mind too much. I played sad, funny, serious, deluded, old and young women, but being cast as the gangster's moll, a lady with a gun and of decidedly easy virtue in *Ghost Train*, I felt that the deterioration had eventually gone far enough.

Drawing on my limited experience of production, in a weak moment I volunteered to produce a school play. At assembly, the head announced that anyone who wished to take part should be in the hall straight after lunch. This resulted in three jeering boys making faces through the windows and the whole of the rest of the school waiting with anticipation for their chance to tread the boards.

I had decided on *Sleeping Beauty*. I would tell the story and when I came to a character which appealed to anyone, they could go over to Pam and she would put their name in the appropriate slot. All went well, with a unanimous consensus over the part of Sleeping Beauty, an outstandingly pretty girl with long, golden hair and not a conceited bone in her body.

A friend had offered to get me some very fine strands of a thread which would be excellent for representing cobwebs so there were some volunteers to play the spiders who would spin this over the sleeping cast. A loud murmur of approval went up as two sisters and their friend, all of Afro-Caribbean extraction went excitedly to volunteer.

There were comments from the others such as, "Cor, Miss, won't they be great as the spiders?" and "Just think of them in their black leotards. They'll be great!"

The approval for these three was so unanimous, that no-one else asked to be considered as spiders and three happy girls looked forward to their parts.

The next day, I was just clearing up ready to go home, when the head asked me to go to his room. As I entered, I met the furious gaze of one of the black mothers whom I knew vaguely by sight. The head tried to put the problem to me, but the woman made it loudly clear that she considered me a racist, a bigot, a spiteful woman who should never even think of being a teacher when I was so totally biased against anyone from an ethnic minority. Thinking past the rather disjointed accusations, I gathered that she was under the impression that I had picked on her two daughters and their friend because they were black. She paused for breath, giving me a chance to explain that, far from being picked on her daughters had secured the parts in our play that they wanted and as everyone thought how good they were they had gone away delighted.

Disbelief was written on her face and she flounced off, accompanied by her daughters who were both sobbing with disappointment at their mother's assertion that they would not be in the play. This situation persisted and although we had stand-ins as spiders at the rehearsals, there was great rejoicing amongst all of us when, two days before the first performance, the mother relented and the three beautiful black girls became the favourite actresses. I took it that I was forgiven when they presented me with a posy of flowers from their mother, who sat in the front row and became liberally festooned with fine threads by her triumphant daughters.

What a shame that the older generations try to resurrect divisions because of religion, skin colour or background when children are generally so accepting of them.

LAMENT FOR THE TURKEY

"Will you walk across the farmyard?" said the turkey to the hen.
"There are things I ought to tell you of perfidy of men.

"Do you realise they use you and will never set you free?
They let you lay your children, then they eat them for their tea."

"However can I thank you?" replied the silly hen.
"Stop laying eggs," said turkey. "Deprive those greedy men."

For forty days the obedient hen did what the turkey said
And, horrifically egg-bound, she soon was lying dead.

"Will you walk across the farmyard?" said the turkey to the bull.
"Did you know you're only kept here because your quiver's
full?"

"Is that a fact?" the great beast roared. (His voice surpassed his
  brain.)
"I really thought it was for love I'd see my cows again."

"Not so," the helpful turkey said. "You're good at just one thing.
To leave the present treadmill you've got to act the king.

"Act all fierce, refuse to be a big obedient beast."
And so it was that Sunday's lunch was such a beefy feast.

"Will you trot across the farmyard?" said the turkey to the
    horse.
"I think that you're intelligent. You can't be fooled, of course.

"But surely you must realise, surely you are able
To see you're kept on sufferance in a warm and comfy stable.

"Just think of when the Master's weight is too much for your
    back
When hair falls out of tail and mane and all your teeth turn
    black."

Which frightened poor old Dobbin so, he got St Vitus' dance
Was shot, and got turned into glue and tasty steaks in France.

"Now at this rate," the turkey thought, "I soon shall reign
    supreme.
There's ducks and geese and pigs and goats, and cows providing
    cream."

And so he set about the task, extinguishing the lot. . . .
But just too late, it's Christmas Eve. It's *his* turn for the pot.

LASTING MEMORIES

No matter the reason or how early or late a teacher retires, there are incidents which remain in the memory forever.

I cannot forget the beautiful chestnut-coloured bullrushes given to me by a friend and which gave such pleasure to all in the unit. Bullrushes are probably the most tactile of plants and their soft brown stems just asked to be stroked. Anything which encouraged a gentle, caring touch was most welcome, as so many of those who came to us had never known gentleness and could often soften for the first time towards something furry.

In my ignorance, I left the dark stems on the window sill when we left school one Friday afternoon. On Monday morning, we lined up, as usual, ready to go into the classroom. On opening the door with one hand, Pam grabbed me with the other. Behind her, an enormous silky cloud floated gently to and fro in the slight breeze from the open door. To our sadness, our beautiful bullrushes were gone; just bare, gaunt stalks remained. Even the excitement of chasing and collecting the velvety remains failed to assuage the feeling of loss, for it brought upon all of us the transient nature of lovely things.

With many of the children in the unit having experienced, to some degree, the harsh side of life, it was important to show them that gentleness, both given and received, were to be prized. At first, so many could not bear to be touched and yet in time found a cuddle a great comfort. It really gave us a feeling of achievement when a previously alienated child, who had wrung our hearts with their silent sadness, reached out to us or to their companions, mentally and physically. To aid this development, I felt that a small, furry creature which had been hand-trained would be a welcome addition to the classroom. My son had completely tamed a lovely little hamster which was covered in soft golden fur. As well as the purpose for which it had originally been intended, it worked wonders for formal education as well as the more important aspects of learning. When a child had finished all three pieces of required work each day and could therefore choose an occupation, playing with the hamster became a favourite and definitely speeded up the rate of work required to complete required tasks.

There appeared a myriad of ways in which the tiny creature brought its benefits. The one girl who was with us at that time and who never addressed a word to another human being, whispered for hours to the hamster, unaware that at the same time it frequently concentrated on stuffing parts of her dress or her jumper into its cheeks. The boys delighted in making houses and complicated runs for the little creature and invariably showed how gentle and considerate they could be.

The hamster came home with me each holiday, as to allow it to go to a home where I knew little of the circumstances may have proved harmful, if not fatal. There were some families who could have been trusted, but if they were allowed a temporary hamster lodger, I would have had to do the same for all the children in turn, so it was safer to take it to and fro with me. I should have done the same at the weekends, for one Monday morning we arrived at school to find the cage empty, with the latch neatly undone. We looked everywhere within the classroom, then around the rest of the school, but there was no sign of our little Houdini. That night and every consequent night and weekend we left the cage door open and a tasty heap of food within, but to no avail. By the end of the term we had to accept that Hammy had found a life elsewhere. It was many months before the staff learnt about his end and we did not sully the children's happy memories with the murderous news.

Some time later Mr Watts, feeling moved to tell the school about some world event, delved into his large cardboard box where his big maps were stored. The children were, as usual, enthralled with his story as he unrolled the world map which was secured to a frame at the top with drawing pins. The head swept across the map with a suitable worldwide flourish, oceans and continents appearing in all their technicolour glory – but the Antarctic was not there. The chart ended in a frilly edge rather than the southern end of our planet.

The disappearance was a mystery until the caretaker volunteered that he had observed what he took to be rat droppings round the school during the half-term holiday. He had secured the services of the 'Rodent Officer' who had put down poison at points in the open so that every scrap could be cleared before the school was opened again. So ended our little friend, although I let the fading memory take its course rather than divulge the truth to the children. If they read this, they will be quite old enough by now to learn the true facts.

Two incidents which could have been avoided if parents had complied with school rules caused unnecessary injuries to two children. There was a fashion for wooden-soled shoes which had only fronts to them and otherwise nothing to keep them on children's feet. Apart from the noise of several pairs of this type of footwear clumping along stone corridors and up and down concrete staircases, they were an obvious danger, offering no support to the wearer or to those who tripped over them as they were regularly shed anywhere in the building or playground. To prevent inevitable accidents, headteachers in the city banned the wearing of this totally unsuitable footwear from their schools. One mother, who took this pronouncement to be a condemnation of the way she chose to dress her daughter and an intrusion on her parental rights refused to comply. First thing in the morning, the girl attempted to mount the concrete stairs, her shoe slipped sideways, taking with it her leg which jammed in the bannisters while she fell further down. The compound break in her leg took months to mend and we felt sorry for a child who had had to suffer because of a parent's resentful thoughtlessness.

For that same reason, despite a school rule allowing only small studs, another girl was sent to school wearing large, hoop earrings. A qualified teacher had to be present while a student on school practice took the class for gymnastics. As it would give my unit children an extra treat, I volunteered to combine both classes. The student was instructed by the class teacher to get her class changed into their PE kit and to keep them in the entrance hall until I joined her. I arrived at the door of the hall just in time to see children milling about amongst the gymnastic equipment and the girl, still wearing her hooped earrings, climbing the wall bars.

I arrived to witness the consternation of the student as she saw the result of her lax discipline and disregard for long-established rules. A pushing contest amongst children who had rushed, unsupervised, into the hall resulted in the earringed girl losing her grip on the bars, leaving one of her hoops hooked over the top fixing. I have never seen so much blood. The girl's mother claimed that her daughter insisted on wearing the hoops to school and would not be dissuaded, but the girl said her mother had never tried to stop her wearing them. Unfortunately it was the youngster who suffered again, yet it is surprising how many parents refuse to see the safety implications of what their children wear at school, putting fashion or persuasion before security.

School sports days were great fun, with the accent firmly on fun rather than competitiveness, with members of staff joining in and the head, resplendent in yachting hat, opening the batting in what always turned into a comedy cricket match. Looking back, it seems as if on all sports days the sun shone from a totally blue sky, but true memory recalls that sports days could be postponed until the weather was kind to us.

One April 1st, we were all summoned to the school hall and, when seated and quite quiet, told that the Queen had sent a solemn message to all schools. She had a foreign visitor come to England from a land far away and she wanted to show him how appreciative she was that he had travelled so far to see her. In his honour, therefore, we were to sing his national anthem. However, the original tune was very complicated, so Her Majesty had offered to lend him her tune and he had graciously accepted.

All the children stood respectfully as Mr Watts pointed to the board where he had printed the words of the song in large letters.

Our music specialist sat reverently at the piano. All the children, looking most impressed, sang with concentration to the tune of 'God Save Our Gracious Queen'

> *Oh, wattan Ah Siam, Oh wattan Ah Siam,*
> *Oh wattan Ah.*
> *Oh wattan Ah Siam, Oh wattan Ah Siam,*
> *Oh wattan Ah Siam, Oh wattan Ah.*

I felt inordinately proud that it was a child in my unit who was the first to realise what they were singing and who was falling about with laughter while the rest were still solemnly declaring their loyal welcome.

To an outsider, this could, perhaps have appeared to be a waste of time, but wise teachers know that the generation of such fun under controlled conditions creates a happy atmosphere and a willingness to cooperate in the learning of what is required. Those who were there at the time still mention it and we laugh together again when I meet them after many years.

I hear about some of my 'graduates' now and again. In some cases a family's habitual and criminal occupation was inescapable and claimed the next generation for its way of life. The arts of thieving and deception had been passed down for generations and parents were loath to see the technique forgotten. In less civilised times these attributes could have spelled the difference between life and death and played upon the natural instincts of survival, so that morality still vies with instinct.

While my grandparents were alive, it was a terrific asset to consult them about the history of the family of which a small member was to enter my class. Having lived and taught in the city and knowing of the residents long before that, when news of one's environment travelled remarkably quickly by word of mouth, Grandpa Eric and Grandma Ette Keys were founts of information. Before the number of the city's population exploded, I only had to mention the surnames of my expected pupils to gain invaluable information about the family backgrounds. Sometimes the information I fed back caused great surprise, for families who had, only two generations ago, been pushing barrows and crying "rags, bones" throughout the suburban roads now ran lucrative antique businesses or fashionable dress boutiques and attended such places as Ascot. One third-generation member, from a pitifully poor background in the historically worst slum dwellings in Gloucester, had graciously donated so much of his mysteriously acquired fortune to good causes that he obtained a summons to be invested with an appropriate award at Buckingham Palace.

These were notable exceptions to the usual, pedestrian information, but interesting to us as a family and it all added up to a greater understanding of each child. My grandparents took with them a valuable asset to the teaching they left behind.

I grieve for those children who have passed through my hands and who have now passed on to what one hopes will be a better life. I think of the blonde, mop-haired boy who joined in a game of 'chicken' on the bypass round the city but was not so nimble as the others; it was heartbreaking to watch his mother's grief at his funeral. I could never forget the tiny girl, the sole daughter of a couple who had longed for a child and whose small body, supported by mine, had trembled with joy when the Queen visited the city. Each school was allotted a space in the park, but leukaemia had made little Rosie terminally ill and much too weak to attend school. The headmaster fetched her and took her home afterwards, but her delighted cry of "The Queen, the Queen" echoed in our memories for a long time.

I remember the handsome teenager whose epilepsy medication was allowed to lapse and who died falling from a train; the girl too frightened to speak until she felt sufficiently secure to express herself; those children who were, sadly, destined to follow their forebears' precarious way of life which leads to prison and a waste of humanity. So many, and all individuals with so much potential.

Special education and, specifically the special unit, were created to enable disadvantaged children to realise their inherent possibilities and to increase the possibility of a happy, fulfilled life. I feel privileged to have been a small part of that.

Every child with whom I have come into contact throughout my varied career has claimed a small place in my heart, but it is those who for many differing reasons have suffered emotionally, physically and, consequentially educationally who have presented the biggest challenges.

Inevitably, they have afforded me the greatest satisfaction and for that I owe them an enormous debt of gratitude.

AMEN

Aged eight, survivor of unspeakable abuse.
Tousle-haired, knobby-kneed,
Ragged dress, broken sandals,
Runs through a meadow ablaze with flowers,
Leaps into the air with sheer joy and shouts,
"Thank you, God, for a lovely world."

WISHES DO COME TRUE

Seven days before Christmas, yet still in his bed
Father Christmas was sleeping. "Get up," his wife said.

The elves had worked hard, making thousands of toys,
But how would they get to the good girls and boys?

Up through the ether from dozens of homes
Came selfish requests to the hard-working gnomes.

"I want a computer," demanded the brat,
But Santa ignored him for shouting like that.

'Twas six days, then five days, then four days, then three
And the baubles and tinsel were hung on the tree.

Only two days to go now and Christmas Day loomed,
The sledge ready oiled and the eight reindeer groomed.

"I'm sick of the grasping, I'll not go this year,"
Yet as Santa grumbled, what did he hear?

Amidst all the grabbing and raucous demands,
A little girl whispered, clasping her hands,

"Please, don't bring me presents – I'm feeling too sad.
Just something for Mummy – and bring home my Dad."

Fast as a rocket, Santa leapt out of bed.
"There's no time for breakfast. Hitch the reindeer," he said.

They flew like the wind all the way to Iraq
To find the girl's Daddy and bring him straight back.

'Twas the night before Christmas – and give him his due,
Father Christmas is proof that wishes come true.

"PLAN THE FUTURE BY THE PAST"
(Burke)

The chronic back injury I sustained in a road traffic accident abruptly ended my teaching career, but in one respect it did me a favour, for it saved me from the straightjacket of the National Curriculum, which became obligatory a short time afterwards. I fear that it would have gradually sapped my natural enthusiasm.

Having tried knitting for export, which was possible while my back partially mended, I discovered that my labour was rewarded with the paltry payment of just over 11p an hour, but still having partially to support my two sons, I responded to requests to tutor local children who were struggling at school. It was apparent that their problems very often arose from dyslexia, giving me the added interest of teaching children who learn and think like I still do.

From this came the formation of the local branch of the Dyslexic Association, with thriving workshops, staffed by specialist teachers, in the local library as well as a continual need for my diagnostic services. We were proud to receive Queen's Anniversary Silver and Bronze awards for our achievement.

Some parents required individual tuition for their severely dyslexic children. This I undertook with pleasure, as I greatly missed being with and helping children.

Meantime, the educational games I had devised over the years were first produced by Bath Educational Publishers, then by the LDA of Cambridge who distributed them throughout the country. With the advent of the National Curriculum I was asked to adapt them to the new requirements. This I did gladly, as a means of bringing some fun to learning to read. Later, more equipment was added to the LDA list, under my registered name of Happy Learning.

Not having learnt to read or, of course, write, until I was eight years old I had little outlet for a vivid imagination. My first efforts at writing were disparaged by teachers who thought that caning and thumping would, miraculously, 'cure' what was being called word blindness . Thankfully, the eleven-plus exam, did not rely solely on correct spelling and I entered one of the wonderful grammar schools which Gloucester still proudly possesses. There, abilities were sought and encouraged, although I was determined not to follow in the footsteps of most of my forebears; I would become *anything* rather than a teacher. The days I spent with Miss Cleverly in her special school completely changed my attitude, for in a way I sensed that I had come home.

I was barely eighteen when I applied to Fishponds Training College and heard immediately that there was one place vacant in the nursery/infant course. I could start in the following September and that training was invaluable, for if you know what has come before in a child's life, you can build on it. The rest you have just read about.

Over the years, I have had poems published in the local and national press and in many British anthologies. I have included a few to form breaks in the concentrated life which is education.

Two university courses in original writing reawakened my interest in the subject so that I became a member of the prestigious Cotswold Writers' Circle and now lead a small group who enjoy writing for fun.

I hope you enjoyed reading this book as much as I enjoyed writing it. It is dedicated to all those children who, through many years, have taught me so much. Thank you.

ASSESSMENT OF THE EDUCATIONAL WORK OF UNA DOWDING
by an educational psychologist, BA, DipEd, MEd, MA, FBPsS

This is no experiment in scatter-brained ideas.

Una is a teacher of almost countless years' experience.

She has taught the 'quick learner', the 'slow learner', the placid and the wild, the rough and the very smooth.

Her work has always been centred on the learning of reading and she has accomplished through her approach the most outstanding results.

Children not only want to learn, they come knocking on her door demanding the chance to PLAY!

Teachers are often daunted by the task of 'teaching children to read'. Now the whole process becomes enjoyable.

Parents will grab at it, open-handed, for at last the chance to enjoy 'homework' with the child.

If you can't spell, there are spellchecks and dictionaries.

If you can't cope with maths, there are calculators and computers.

If you can't read, you are a dependant for life.